Dedication

I would like to dedicate this book to my mom for all her love and support both in life and the afterlife.

Acknowledgement

I would like to thank my wife and twin flame, Kate, for without her editing and creative writing my book would not have taken form. Special thanks to my sister, Sharon, for her encouragement and to all my brothers and sisters for their willingness to share their stories. To my daughter, Courtenay, for her typing and spell checking.

Thank you to Greg Pauker for coaching me through the process of making the Creative Meditation CD that is included with this book. Also thanks for the mixing and mastering this CD. Also to John Malcolm of Barnyard Grafix for layout, design and printing of this book.

Table of Contents

Introduction

When I was twelve years old I went to a bookstore with my mom and picked out a book that I wanted to read. Someone standing close by remarked to my mother, "I wouldn't let my son read that book." Lucky for me my mom had a less critical view of my choice. She simply replied, "he's not your son" then turned and paid for the book. The subject of the book was hypnosis and even then I was fascinated with hypnosis, magic and psychic abilities. As a teenager I spent a lot of time practicing magic and reading books on the supernatural. I could understand that we had a conscious mind and I understood how we could have a sub-conscious, but the concept of a collective or universal mind, I couldn't grasp. It wouldn't be until much later in life with the help of quantum physics that I would understand the power of this universal mind. For some reason even at twelve I knew I wanted to develop physic abilities and teach others to do the same. Now at the age of 38 and with the experience of my many life lessons, I feel I'm finally starting to do that.

My vision of the future is one where this information is easily understood and a part of our everyday lives. That's why I believe it is important to get this information out there as much as possible. Until we have heard enough, experienced enough, and believe enough to know we are "spiritual beings having a human experience" and live our lives accordingly. There are many books you can read on these subjects some are more complex than others. I have tried to simplify these concepts as best as I can so that all can benefit from understanding the workings of our inner mind. The key to self discovery is learning to be your true self. Taking the time to do that and using the tools I talk about in the book is the choice and the challenge you have to make.

"Treat the earth well:
it was not given to you by your parents,
it was loaned to you by your children.
We do not inherit the Earth from our Ancestors,
we borrow it from our children.

Ancient Proverb

Chapter 1

Theory
of the Mind

*"We are more than the sum of our knowledge,
we are the products of our imagination."*

Ancient Proverb

Every now and then go away, have a little

relaxation, for when you come back to your

work your judgment will be surer.

Go some distance away because then the work

appears smaller and more of it can be taken in

at a glance and a lack of harmony and

proportion is more readily seen.

Leonardo da Vinci

I call it "theory of the mind," because things are always changing. Our perception is always expanding. It was not long ago that we thought the world was flat and that the sun circled the earth, today we know the earth is not flat, and in fact it circles the sun. I wonder how we will see things 100 years from now?? How will we have changed physically and more importantly spiritually? In the first few chapters, I'll endeavor to explain the workings of the physical body and brain. As the book progresses you'll see that we are so much more than flesh and blood bodies. Our body is simply the vehicle that our spirit chose to grow and develop from. To begin, however, I think it is important to understand what we know today about the workings of our minds and our bodies.

Science teaches us that every living thing in the universe is energy moving atoms. When these atoms orbit at high-speed they appear to be solid but in actuality they are not really solid at all. We are 99.999% energy and .001 percent physical atoms. The organization of these atoms creates our physical reality. Our bodies form a physical flesh and blood vehicle through the complex organization of these atoms. These atoms form cells and cells form organs, each cell acts like a computer chip storing and processing emotions and thoughts. All of our body parts create electromagnetic fields. Modern science uses equipment like EEG and biofeedback machines to measure these electrical fields. The complexity of these fields creates an intricate system of communication both conscious and unconscious. In turn, these systems regulate blood pressure, oxygen flow and regeneration of the cells. All of our experiences and memories are stored in and through every part of us, in every cell and tissue.

Simply put, I believe when you were born and took your first breath of life your circuits were turned on. You started to record everything that happened to you. You started to develop beliefs about your world based on your experiences. The information you collected was stored in your mind and body's energy fields. In the late 1700's Anton Mesmer, a Viennese physician, believed disease was caused by an imbalance in a person's magnetic fluid (energy field). He used hypnotic trance to balance their mental and emotional state, which would often result in healing. It is amazing to think that Mesmer saw the body as being made up of magnetic fluid as early as the 1700's. He was on the right track for sure. Now over 200 years later we know electromagnetic fields of energy do indeed regulate our bodies and our minds.

As I mention often in this book, in the same way that you don't have to understand the inner workings of a computer to use it, you don't have to understand the complexity of the mind to use it. However, you need to know enough about how it works in order to believe it will.

The mind uses the cerebral cortex of the brain, the twin hemispheres, as its tools. These two hemispheres coordinate the entire organism. The left hemisphere of the brain is more focused on the physical world. Its' functions are logical and systematic, concerned more with matters of concrete reality. The right brain concentrates on what we would call non-logical thinking--intuition, feeling and emotions. It uses images [pictures] for communication. Synchronizing our left and right hemispheres allows us to access more of our subconscious mind. This process has long been associated with meditation and hypnologic states. Particularly in our western culture there has been an over emphasis on the logical left brain. Over emphasis on logic without an allowance for intuition blocks our natural right brain functions. Right brain non-logical intuition is culturally suppressed in us as children. Non-logical information is present all the time by our right brain. Mystics explain that by slowing down our left hemisphere, our right intuitively perceives. It's also essential that the left brain logical mind has an understanding of the right brains abilities in order to use this information.

Left Hemisphere	Right Hemisphere
• *Logic*	• *Emotion*
• *Words*	• *Creativity*
• *Detail*	• *Pictures*

Creative Meditation uses mental intention and breath in order to slow down our minds and allow the two hemispheres to come together. Biofeedback machines able to measure brain wave frequencies explain it this way. Brain waves, or the EEG are electrical signals that can be recorded from the brain by hooking up wires to the scalp. The electrochemical activity of the brain results in the production of electromagnetic waves from which we can measure and objectively study. This breakthrough came in the 1940's when Hans Berger, a German scientist, discovered the brain wave states of Beta and

Alpha. After placing electrodes on the scalp of a subject, his galvanometer showed electrical activity. Further studies showed the presence of two distinct states. One associated with being awake and alert (beta) and the other a more creative or passive state known as (alpha). While you are physically alert the mind is in Beta. While in the state of Beta one experiences a sense of being controlled by time and space. You can only stay in this alert state for a couple of hours before your mind needs to download into a more relaxed state known as Alpha. This slower brain wave state brings an increased feeling of relaxation and creativity. Studies have shown that we instinctively move into a healing state of mind called the Ultradian Response every 90 minutes. In this state the right hemisphere of the brain is more active than normal because we have moved from Beta to Alpha. You may have noticed that every couple of hours you need to rest or that your mind can't stop daydreaming. This daydreaming and tiredness shows you that your mind is sorting out information. Further research in this area detected two more brain wave states known as Theta and Delta. As you fall asleep at night your mind enters an even slower brain wave state known as Theta. Information stored in the more conscious states of Beta and Alpha now slips into Theta. Theta is associated with the beginning stages of sleep and the dream state. Rem sleep or dreaming occurs in the theta state. The muscles of the body are paralyzed, however the heartbeat and respiratory systems act as they would during emotional upsets in waking life. Theta is the gateway to sleep. Delta is the state we reach when we fall into a deep sleep. There is further slowing down of mental vibrations. Delta is thought to be a time of rejuvenation and healing, while we sleep our endocrine organs come to life and secrete hormones into the bloodstream that affect the whole body. This is a period of regeneration and cell renewal, and without sufficient Theta and Delta sleep, one can suffer from sleep deprivation. These brain wave states represent levels of our conscious and sub-conscious mind. All your past experiences and past memories are stored at different levels of the mind, Delta, Theta and part of Alpha. The states of Delta and Theta reflect your sub-conscious mind. Beta reflects your conscious mind and Alpha is the link between them. As you developed from a baby to an adult your brain waves were developing with you. From birth to about age three we function from the Delta State. All of our early experiences are recorded and stored at this level. As the years go on Theta develops, creating more of a separation between conscious and subconscious mind. By your teen-age years you have developed all four levels. You can see that experiences and information that you have retained are stored at different brain wave states as you grow up. It starts to make sense why most of us can't remember things when we were very young, because this information is stored in the unconscious state of Delta. These early memories are still with us and do affect us, but are not usually conscious. Through meditation or hypnosis we can retrieve memories from these states. Meditation is the ability to move into a relaxed mental state of Alpha. In Alpha the mind has access to the subconscious and the conscious at the same time. The left and right hemispheres of your brain start hemming as it's called. They work in sync creating a powerful tool for self-discovery. All cultures throughout time have intuitively developed methods to create these trance experiences. They use breath, sound, incense, ritual, dance, drumming, fasting, pain, and guided imagery to move themselves into an Alpha or Theta state. Yogi masters train themselves to raise their body temperature enough to melt snow. In scientific tests it has been shown that these masters can take themselves into Theta and even Delta. From these states it is not only possible to raise body temperature, they can also control all sorts of bodily functions. In deep hypnosis people have been known to have successful operations without the use of anesthetic. Anton Mesmer was the one to arouse the scientific community with his experiments in this field. Through his knowledge and belief in animal magnetism and suggestion he cured hundreds if not thousands of people. His fundamental belief in the 1700's was that disease was caused by an imbalance in a person's magnetic fluid. By taking them into trance [alpha or theta] and through the power of suggestion he was able to balance their mental and emotional state. Today science knows we have electromagnetic fields of energy that regulate our bodies and minds. Kerling photography and sensitive equipment can photograph and read these energy fields. I imagine a day not much different than Star Trek, when we will be able to detect disease and cure it from these energy states. It is very important to get Alpha rest and be aware of the natural cycle of the Ultradain Response. The Ultradain Response means every 90 to 120 minutes our mind spontaneously moves into an Alpha state in order to download or sort out information. If you don't allow your mind to relax like this you become what is known as hyper suggestible. In other words your conscious (Beta State) can no longer hold any more information. If your Beta State becomes over-loaded everything that happens to you or is said to you goes into your sub-conscious mind. As a result, it becomes difficult to handle your environment; you may feel frustrated and even a little crazy at times. We also have a secondary Beta state that is from 20 to 40 hertz. This is when the mind is racing. This usually happens at night when we can't stop worrying about events from the day. Biofeedback research on Alpha training has been very effective at teaching people how to slow their mind's down. The research showed that people who trained themselves to slow their mind's down had great success with overcoming chemical dependencies, eating disorders, post traumatic stress, panic attacks and even multiple personalities. So proper Alpha rest, daydreaming and physical rest are essential for clear thinking and a healthy body. In the next chapter and on my CD Creative Meditation, I'll teach you a variety of relaxation and breathing techniques. In a very short period of time you'll be able to use this creative healing state at will. An easy way to slow your mind down to Alpha is to take a walk in nature. Researchers have found that the earth sends out a resonance wave of 7.8 Hz, which is the same frequency as Alpha. The soothing rhythm of ocean waves, the peacefulness of the forest, all help slow our mind down to Alpha. There are some theories that suggest our brains may be phase-locked in some way with the earth and it's atmosphere. On a chemical level your brain cells reset their sodium and potassium ratios when the mind is in deep alpha or theta. Sodium and potassium are the chemicals involved in transporting other chemicals in and out of our brain cells. A brief meditation of 5 to 15 minutes restores this balance. The result is a feeling of calm and rejuvenation.

Now we have a basic model of how our mind uses brain waves. Beta and part of alpha is our conscious state; alpha is the go between of our sub-conscious and conscious mind, theta and delta reflect our sub-conscious. As we fall asleep at night our day's activities, our thoughts and experiences move into our sub-conscious mind. Dreaming is a reflection of our mind processing information. The mind works in symbols, (pictures) as we dream we're relating our new experiences with past memories. When you learn something new like driving a car, you're in Beta, your nervous etc. As the days and weeks pass, and you process your new experiences through dreaming and daydreaming, your ability to drive a car becomes sub-conscious. In time you may find that you're driving along and didn't realize that you passed your destination. Your ability to drive is now so unconscious that you can literally do it without conscious thought. This is also how a negative habit is developed. In the chapter to come I'll show you how you can break habits by reconditioning your sub-conscious. Remember brain wave states are a way of objectifying our minds. They are not our minds. Beta, Alpha, Theta and Delta are what we use to identify changes in consciousness. They are not consciousness in themselves. The same way that our blood pressure tells us something about our hearts, brain waves tell us something about our mind's abilities and the different states we can go into.

BETA   ALPHA   THETA & DELTA

DELTA	*0-4*
THETA	*4-8*
ALPHA	*8-13*
BETA	*13-20*
BETA II	*20-24*

numbers indicate brain wave oscillations per second

DELTA WAVES:

Delta is profound sleep. There is further slowing down of mental vibrations. While in Delta we sort out our mental and physical machinery. This is a period of regeneration and cell renewal. From the ages of 0-3 you are in Delta.

THETA WAVES:

Theta is the portal for entering night-time sleep. We all pass through Theta twice a day. When we fall asleep at night and when we awaken in the morning. We also move in and out of Theta when we dream. From the ages of 3-7 you fluctuate between Theta and Delta.

ALPHA WAVES:

This is the area of the mind which brings increased creativity and physical relaxation. Not only is the level of stress reduced but many people enter a light or hypnotic trance or meditation. At this level there is a slowing down of brain and body pulsation. From the ages of 7-13 you fluctuate between Alpha, Theta, and Delta.

BETA WAVES:

The Beta state is one of physical alertness with mind and emotions responsive to the senses. Most of our waking time is spent in this state which is associated with tension and striving. While in Beta one experiences a sense of being controlled by time and space. From the age of 13 and up you fluctuate between all four levels.

BETA 2:

The Beta 2 state is when your mind is racing and worried about everything. There is a sense of being disconnected from everything. It is not a healthy state to be in. However not everyone experiences this state. It is usually associated with mental fatigue.

Chapter 2

Energy follows Thought

All that we are is the result of
what we have thought.
The mind is everything.
What we think, we become.

Buddha

"Hold a picture of yourself long and steady enough in your mind's eye, and you will be drawn toward it."

Napoleon Hill

"Cherish your visions and your dreams as they are the children of your soul, the blueprints of your ultimate achievements."

Napoleon Hill

The first thing Creative Meditation does is allow you to observe and relax your body. Once you have mastered this physical relaxation you are able to gain greater emotional control. In time you start to feel as though everyday life is slowing down. You feel less and less controlled by habits and outside environment. Your mind is more open to your sub-conscious and your instincts are sharper.

The most important thing to remember is that energy follows thought (as you sow, so shall you reap). Energy goes naturally to the frequencies of your thoughts, the more you think about something the more power it has. This works with negative or positive thinking. By using progressive relaxation techniques you can clear negative or conflicting messages in your mind and relax the body. With a relaxed body and mind your blood pressure and energy systems are normalized. You feel energized and are open for more creativity and insights. At first it may seem a little difficult to relax in this way. I have included a CD with this book to help you get there without difficulty. It is much easier to learn meditation by listening to someone guide you there. On track one of my CD you will find a fifteen minute guided relaxation. Listen to this meditation often and you will find it's like taking a mini vacation. In time you will be able to do this meditation without the help of the CD. As you meditate your mind moves into alpha and possibly theta. While in these brain wave states you have more influence over your mind and body. You will be able to release tension and stress easily. The world outside is viewed by an individual according to his or her belief systems or state of mind. The way we see the world varies from person to person, culture to culture. Our mind works like a filter, seeing what we are conditioned to see. It's like someone shaving their mustache off or changing their hair, and some people don't notice. For example, did you know that when the first large sailing ships came to the Americas, it was only the shamans with their open perception that could see them? Meditation allows us to go beyond our normal perception and open up to new ideas. Meditation develops witness-consciousness; it gives you the feeling of being able to watch your actions, and emotions more objectively.

You will be able to release tension and stress easily. Stress is one of our biggest culprits in our busy lives today. As Freud has suggested tension is a condition that results from the body being barraged by emotional stimulus, which demands action, however the action seldom or never occurs because society will not permit the gravitation of these impulses. These impulses are primitive urges called, fight or flight. When we are in a stressful or threatening situations our primitive mind wants to fight or flight (run away). This is a response all mammals have that is built in for survival and works great in the wild. As humans in a world full of laws and rules these impulses can't be acted on in the same way. However, electrical impulses for fight or flight are still sent to our muscles and we constantly have to override these impulses with our conscious minds, thereby creating tension in our bodies. Sleep is designed to release these conflicts and does to some extent, but chronic fatigue and stress are difficult to release without meditative time. Extreme stress and tension drastically affect the operation of our body's systems. Unconsciously, stress starts to affect blood pressure, heart conditions, and our respiratory system. Our gastrointestinal system can become stressed, which includes your stomach, liver, gall bladder, and intestines. Even your hearing, eye sight, sense of smell and taste can all be affected by stress. Progressive relaxation as shown on track one of my CD is about allowing your mind and body to release this chronic tension.

As I mentioned in Chapter One, disease is usually a result of conflicting emotions that are shorting out some part of our energy systems. Deeply relaxing the body, as we do in meditation, helps restore this balance. Once you have mastered the ability to relax your body and relieve tension, the next step is strengthening your mental skills. Our thoughts create our reality, hard to believe but it's true. All the masters talk of the importance of our thoughts. Energy follows thought. So the more we think about something, the more likely it's going to happen. Focusing our thoughts and visualizing our goals are essential. Track two of the Creative Meditation CD guides you into a meditative state (alpha) where you can begin to visualize your goal. This could be breaking a habit, setting a business or sports goal, or maybe looking for what you want in a relationship. Here's how it works. As you know everything in the universe is energy. Energy moving atoms, organizing events, shaping our self's and our environments. As you focus and concentrate your thoughts you start to direct this energy. In a meditative state you are at the gateway of the sub-conscious mind. As you visualize and affirm goals in this state you are programming your sub-conscious. The sub-conscious then begins to create and direct change in our habits and behaviors. Now remember your sub-conscious energy fields are not limited to your physical body. They interact with the universe in ways we are only beginning to understand. We speak to our sub-conscious mind in images (a picture is worth a 1000 words). Your sub-conscious will focus energy and seek out the experiences you are visualizing. Remember the saying... watch what you ask for because you just might get it. Now you may be saying, I want to be a millionaire and I'm not... so this obviously doesn't work. You have to believe that you will get or create what you are visualizing. The reason that some of the negative or bad things tend to happen to us is that we believe they will. That's not to say that we make bad things happen to us. But if we are conditioned to expect them, they will happen more often. Do you see what I'm saying? You have to think it will happen and then affirm and visualize it. In the meditation I'll have you relax into an alpha state, from there you will visualize and imagine yourself attaining your goals. Psychological studies have shown it takes about three weeks for the sub-conscious to totally accept a new behavior. For habits like smoking or weight loss, it's important to break your habit down. For instance to help you quit smoking, you need to slowly break the habit down. Along with visualizing yourself as a non-smoker, you start to change your habit. Examples like not smoking in the car, on the phone, or not smoking for the first or last hour of the day. Set up a quit date and work towards it. If at first you don't succeed try, try again. For weight loss, change your daily routines. For example; not eating after 8:00 pm or eating fruit in the morning, and drinking lots of water throughout the day. In your meditations, see yourself making small changes every week. In no time at all you will begin to change your body. Don't set yourself up with big expectations, simply do something different everyday and see what happens. Maybe tomorrow you go for a walk at lunch, remember energy follows thought, if you think different, you are different. Along with your daily creative meditation exercises, it's important to use your daydreaming abilities to affirm and visualize your goals. The point of power is in the present moment, so take action. Do things that move you towards your goals. The next time you do your meditation assess the progress you've made and then visualize moving even closer to your goals. Remember the meditative state is a two-way street; so don't be surprised if while visualizing your goals other messages come into your mind. Insights, inspirations or new perceptions about something may come to your awareness. You are in a sub-conscious state, and therefore your creativity and problem solving abilities will be heightened. Research has shown that athletes can improve their game simply by using visualization techniques. Athletes around the world have been using relaxation and visualization for decades now. A university in Europe is using brain wave machines to teach students how to maintain an alpha state of relaxation. Studies are showing that this form of mental training is giving students and athletes a substantial edge. In 1984 Time Magazine reported that woman gymnast, Mary Lou Retton, used visualization (imagery of the mind) to rehearse a perfect routine. She won the gold medal. Sports psychologists say that 80 % of an athlete's performance is in the mind. They are using guided relaxation and visualization for performance enhancement and for fatigue. Athletes are under tremendous stress and physical tension, therefore progressive relaxation is essential. You can see the power creative meditation holds… it gives you the ability to de-stress your mind and body daily, while the power of visualization is in the potential we offer ourselves to improve.

I want to come back now to stress because it has a way of sneaking up on us. Along with your daily meditation it's important to relax throughout the day. If you remember in Chapter One, I talked about the Ultradain Response. This is our natural healing state that happens about every 90 minutes or so. You feel it coming on when your eyes get heavy and it gets hard to concentrate. It's your mind and body's way of downloading thoughts and releasing stress. During this cycle the left and right hemispheres of your brain are hemming (coming together). If you ignore this natural rest cycle, as we so often do, our minds and bodies become overloaded. When your conscious mind (Beta State) becomes overloaded, you don't have the same protection from outside influences or suggestions. In other words, you can't combat negative thoughts. Doing quick relaxations throughout the day allows your mind to download and recharge. On track one of my CD, I showed you a meditation that you can use for relaxation and goals. We can shorten the technique so it takes only minutes to do and yet it rebalances and energizes you throughout the day. This is how it works, when you feel drowsy or tense, close your eyes. Take six or seven deep breaths and try to release your thoughts. Imagine you are at the beach or you're healing pond. Just by closing your eyes you start to move into alpha. From this state it is easy to imagine your healing pond. Deep breathing energizes and clears surface tension also. The breath is a very underrated tool; deep breathing can change our state instantly. There are many different breathing techniques all designed to have a slightly different effect. There are three that I use a lot;

the first is called alpha breathing. This breath is simply in and out through the mouth. When we run we tend to breath in and out through our mouth. It is an instinctive breath that moves us into alpha. Doing this breathing oxygenates your body and moves your mind into alpha effectively clearing your thoughts and emotions. I'm sure you'll be impressed how easy it is to clear emotional frustration using this technique. Next time you feel overwhelmed or frustrated take 15 to 20 deep breaths in and out through your mouth. The breath has amazing power. If you do it as an exercise, try doing it for 10 to 15 minutes, you will be amazed how it energizes your body. People that use these breathing techniques quite often experience a rush of energy coming into their bodies. It is quite a unique experience if it has never happened before. The next exercise I use often is called a cleansing breath. This breath is in through the nose and out through the mouth. It's best to do this breath slow and easy. Count from one to seven on the inhale, hold for three counts and then exhale counting from one to seven, hold for three and start again. You only have to do the counting for a little while in order to get a rhythm.

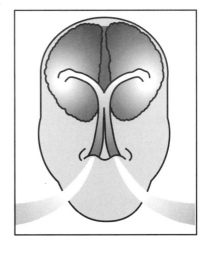

The third exercise I do, but not as often, is nasal breathing. This is when you close off one of your nostrils. The oxygen coming in through the open nostril is cooling that hemisphere of the brain. If you are breathing in through your right nostril you are cooling the right hemisphere of your brain and vice versa. As you know the left and right hemispheres control different aspects of our bodies and mental skills. If you want to feel more creative you would breathe in through your left nasal. If you want to heighten your logical mind you would breathe in through your right nostril. Breath is an easy way to change our consciousness. Explore different breathing techniques and see first hand how powerful it is.

The next point I want to cover is the power of suggestion. Literally, suggestion is the most powerful tool we have. Whether we admit it or not we live our lives by suggestion. Parents, teachers, doctors, news media, preachers, friends and loved ones all make suggestions that influence us throughout our lives. We are constantly being given suggestions whether we want them or not.

The suggestions that we accept or act on directly influence our lives. What we say to ourselves is just as powerful as what we accept from others to guide our lives. Quite often we use negative self talk - I can't do it or I'm not good enough. Unknowingly, we are conditioning our self for lower self-esteem. Simply try to catch yourself and change your perception.

We are our own hypnotists and we hypnotize other people all the time. The definition of hypnosis is the power of suggestion. I've been practicing hypnosis for years now and it is not a state in itself but more the result of compound suggestions. It is suggestions that make the mind manipulate the body. It is suggestion that makes the athlete go the extra mile and it is suggestion that runs our lives. What we say to other people is very powerful as you can see.

Did you know that when someone is crying they are in a hypnotic or suggestible state? That's why when a mother says to her crying child "come here and I'll kiss it better" it usually works. Here is an exercise you can try with a friend using the script provided below. Pick some background music and a quiet environment to take a friend on a guided meditation. Explore the power of your voice, words and compassion to guide this person to a relaxed state. Use the script that I've provided for your first few times, then make up your own. Enjoy!!!

Basic Induction

Before you begin:

1. Sit comfortably in a chair with hands resting on lap.

2. Ask for permission to work with them.

3. State the goal/intention of the session.

Example:

Now I'll ask you to close your eyes and focus on your breathing for a moment. As you do so be aware of all the sounds around you, particularly the sound of my voice. Breathing in slowly, feel a gentle calmness coming in through the eyelids. Your eyelids are the smallest involuntary muscle in your body. Feel how easily you are able to let them go. Sense the warmth and heaviness around them. They are so heavy that they simply won't open. They are getting heavier and heavier as you become calmer and calmer. Now just let go and allow the calm feeling of warmth to flow down through your whole body. You will notice with each and every breath a warm feeling of calmness is coming over you more and more. Now it's moving over your cheeks and jaw. Slowly making its way down your entire body. Feel your neck letting go of all tension. Feel your breath as it moves slowly and peacefully in and out. Feel your chest letting go of all tension as it gently moves in and out. Breathe in the calmness…breathe out the tension. Send that calm, warmth down through your stomach, your hips, thighs, your knees, your calves, your feet and your toes. Feel the tension leave your body as a deep peaceful feeling of calmness takes over. See yourself wrapped in a warm pink blanket. Send that feeling up the back of your legs, your thighs, your buttocks. Letting go of any tension that might be stored there. Especially in the small of your back. We tend to hold a lot of tension there. Feel everything letting go. Moving up the back vertebrae by vertebrae until all the tension is gone. Your entire body feels peaceful, warm and calm.

From this point you can take them on a visualization or use the appropriate suggestions to help them achieve their goal.

Chapter 3

Dreams, Sweet Dreams

A dream is a microscope
through which we look at
the hidden occurrences
in our soul

Erich Fromm

Your visions will become clearer

only when you can look into your own heart.

Who looks outside, dreams;

who looks inside, awakens.

Carl Jung

Learning to remember and interpret our dreams is an exciting and beneficial skill. The people and situations experienced in our dreams show us reflections of unresolved issues, current challenges, and our greatest talents and gifts. With practice we can learn effective and constructive problem solving, how to re-enter our dreams, and even to program our dreams for insights. The first thing you need to do though is to record your dreams in a journal. The mind speaks to us in symbols and it takes time to learn your dream language. However, in time you will start to understand what the symbols mean to you. Some dream analysts believe everything in a dream represents an element inside the dreamer. While there are definitely universal meanings for some symbols, it is wise to try on your own perspectives and look and feel for a connection that is right for you. An easy way to figure out what is special or significant about an image is to contrast it with another image which is similar but different somehow. This technique can give you clues to what your dream is really trying to tell you. For example, if you dream that you are trying to get inside a house by climbing through a tiny window contrast that with using the door instead. Isn't the door much easier? Maybe you are doing something the hard way in your waking reality.

Even though we don't always remember our dreams, we all dream approximately 5-8 times a night. Dreaming is the mind's way of sorting, processing and storing information. The rapid-eye-movement (REM) phase of sleep is where most dreams occur. While we are dreaming, the muscles in our body appear to be paralyzed, while our emotions, heartbeat, and blood pressure act as though we are having the experience. Because our dreams are acted out in this way they are perceived as real experiences by the unconscious mind. Later in this chapter, I'll be showing you a technique called re-dreaming. This technique can be used when you've had a bad or incomplete dream. I have you re-enter your dream and change it. This process is called reframing and is a very useful tool.

There are several different types of dreams such as: premonition, clearing, problem solving and contact from spirit. The first dream of the night usually contains information from your day and is sorting out the mental and emotional clutter. These dreams help us to relax. Premonitions or teaching dreams seem to come in the middle of the night. The early morning dreams are best for basic insight or practical solutions to problems we may be facing. Remember this is a rough outline and only you can decide how meaningful or important each dream is to you. One thing I can guarantee though, is the more you remember your dreams the more you will be amazed at the insights they have for you. When you wake up tomorrow morning, take a moment, close your eyes again and let your mind drift back to what you were dreaming about. Just focusing for a couple of minutes can bring back a dream you might otherwise have lost.

Many aboriginal cultures use dreamtime to face fears. A good example of this is the Senoi Tribe who live in the mountains of Malaysia. In the 1930's Kilton Stewart (an American psychologist) visited the tribe and developed the Senoi Dream Technique.

Senoi Dream Technique

1.   Always confront and conquer the danger in your dreams. If a bear is attacking you in the woods, go toward the bear rather than running from it. If a person strikes you in the dream, fight back, combat and conquer your monsters rather than fearing them.

2.   Always move toward pleasurable experiences in your dreams. If you find yourself flying in a dream, relax and let yourself float on the wind. If you are attracted sexually to an individual in a dream who in the waking world would be taboo for you (your wife's mother, etc,) let yourself enjoy the experience rather than dwell on the negative aspects of the situation.

3.   Always make your dreams have a positive outcome and exact a creative product from them. Seek the poem, painting, song, or other material that can be extracted creatively from the dream. Look for the gift within the imagery. Native American culture teaches the importance of facing animals in our dreams. They believe these spirits are our animal totems and must be confronted without fear in order to make them our friends and protectors.

4.   Facing our fears in our dreams changes our behavior in real life. In hypnotherapy we have people face their fears in a dream like fashion. This process is called desensitization. Having people face their fears in hypnosis or by re-dreaming gives them the ability to reprogram their sub-conscious mind. Many dreams are incomplete, you remember them but can't make any sense of them. Use the following technique to recall your dream and

sort it out. Like in hypnosis, I have you finish the dream, face your fears and resolve any conflicts. This re-dreaming technique is similar to the Senoi Dream Technique in the sense that is allows you to control your dream. If you have nightmares of being chased by something you can re-dream it and confront this fear.

Re-dreaming Meditation

You can use the meditations on your CD or guide yourself into a meditation. I usually use this meditation just after I wake up, so it's easy to remember my dream and easy to slip into a meditative state.

1. Guide yourself into a meditation.
2. Remember all aspects of your dream.
3. Guide yourself through the dream, trying to interpret your dream symbols.
4. Change the dream. If the dream is incomplete or frightening, change it.

The mind doesn't totally recognize a real or imagined event. By visualizing or re-dreaming a positive outcome you change your emotional and mental state. This exercise encourages you to start to lucid dream. Lucid dreaming is when you recognize you are dreaming during a dream and you can control your dream and its course of action. In lucid dreaming, re-dreaming or in hypnosis we have conscious control to create change. The ability for insights, guidance and problem solving in our dreams is enormous. Albert Einstein gives partial credit for his theory of relativity to his dreams. The inventor of the sewing machine [Elias Howe] couldn't figure out how to thread the needle of the sewing machine. In a dream he saw a spear with a hole through the sharp end, this dream gave him the answer to his problem. It is also possible to program your subconscious mind as you fall asleep at night. First of all, take yourself into a light meditative state by breathing deeply for a few minutes. This is the same state you enter just before you fall asleep. Ask your inner guidance for a dream about a particular situation or problem. It is important to trust that your answer will come to you in your dreams. If it does not come the first night, maybe you need to change your question and try

31

again. Remember your question should always pertain to insights about yourself not others. When interpreting your dreams, first decide what type of dream it is. Is it a clearing dream or is it a premonition? Remember although premonition dreams do occur, they are not that common. However some people seem to be more prone to this type of dream. The most common dreams are problem solving which come from our own unconscious or collective minds. These dreams offer us insight and guidance into our everyday life. They offer us strength and purpose. Genesis in the bible is full of dreams believed to be messages from God. Aboriginal cultures today still believe their dreams and visions are messages from the spirit world.

Our subconscious and unconscious are always trying to organize and synchronize our lives. Scientists are working on developing quantum computers that can calculate more steps then there are atoms in the universe. We are always connected to this quantum computer and with the right software (belief system) we can gain great insight from it. Our sub-atomic selves do have the capability to create, plan and problem-solve events. Dreams are a very ancient instinctive part of our minds that when taken serious give us a whole new depth to life. Start by writing your dreams out, everything you can remember. Sometimes it's helpful to meditate on your dream in order to remember more of it. Identify the aspects of the dream that stand out the most. Most dream interpreters see everything in the dream as an aspect of your self. For instance, if you were dreaming of a house everything in the dream represents you. The basement of the house is your subconscious while the kitchen represents how you nurture your self. The attic is your higher awareness, quite often our higher awareness is still unconscious to us. Nightmares or scary dreams are not necessarily bad, they can be showing you new aspects of your self as well. For instance, dreams of a large spider attacking you would be scary, but the spiders are archetypes from your unconscious and like animal totems are there to guide you. In dreams like this you are being shown that you're going through big changes. Spiders are organized, patient creators that continuously work at making their webs. So if you dream of spiders don't be scared, get organized instead. The bedroom usually relates to your relationship with your mate or with your self at some level. Bathroom dreams seem to relate to our physical or emotional state. Dreams of an unclean or backed up toilet etc. would show a need for emotional or physical relief of some kind. Your backyard shows the parts of your self that you don't always want to share with the world. A vehicle in a dream, like the house, tells us something about our waking life. It doesn't matter what vehicle you're in, you want to know if you were driving the car or not. Were you in control of the vehicle in the dream? If you were not, take a look at what is going on in your life.

Remember it doesn't have to be a big thing that's out of control. Maybe you just had a disagreement with someone at work or home. Flying dreams are very common and show at a very basic level our self-confidence. If you're having problems flying in your dreams it may reflect a frustration or insecurity in your life. If you become aware that you're dreaming, use your awareness to make the dream lucid. Like the children of Senoi in Malaysia consciously controlling your dreams increases your confidence in real life. Practice the re-dreaming meditation, this meditation will help condition your mind to remember your dreams and how to control them.

Dream Principles

1. All dreams have a meaning and we all dream.

2. Dreams are a natural means of processing information and are a link to our unconscious.

3. What we can't deal with in our daily lives we live out in our dreams.

4. Dreams are as ancient as humans and offer us messages from our creator self's or god.

5. Re-dreaming, as the Senoi do, is an effective way to clear fears and emotional conflicts

6. There are different types of dreams:

   a. Clearing

   b. Problem solving

   c. Premonition

   d. Contact from spirit

   e. Inner guidance

7. You can program your mind to problem solve in your dreams.

Chapter 4

Contact from Spirit

The breeze at dawn has secrets to tell you.
Don't go back to sleep.
You must ask for what you really want.
Don't go back to sleep.
People are going back and forth across
the doorsill where the two worlds touch.
The door is round and open.
Don't go back to sleep.

Rumi

"To fear death is nothing other than to think

oneself wise when one is not.

For it is to think one knows what one

does not know.

No one knows whether death may not

even turn out to be the greatest blessing

of human beings.

Any yet people fear it as if they knew for certain

it is the greatest evil."

In this chapter I would like to share with you one of the reasons why I chose to look deeper into the unknown and mysterious world of spirit. I was always somewhat interested then something happened that eventually led me to delve into the spirit world in a much bigger way. We all have stories to tell, big or small, events that changed our lives, stories of sadness and of joy. This is my story, the one that changed my life.

My family has been in the food business (grocers) ever since I can remember. My dad and his brothers were in it together. Having come from humble beginnings they were taught to work hard, and look out for each other. Dad, his brothers and his life-long friend Ken Cooper owned a large business and the pressures over the years were quite intense. They had a series of setbacks that eventually led to financial problems. The stress this created was starting to take its toll on my dad. He was in and out of the hospital a few times for mental fatigue and still his behavior was becoming more and more paranoid. The doctors said he was suffering from sleep deprivation due to chronic stress and he was on the verge of having a nervous breakdown. Mom thought a holiday would help ease some of the pressure they were under. None of us knew he was as sick as he was and what happened next changed our reality forever. While on vacation he hit a breaking point and there was nothing that could be done. I'm sure if anyone could have helped dad it would have been my mom. There was no question that they loved each other very much. But I guess that was not meant to be. My dad lost control of his mind, paranoid schizophrenic they called it, and he killed mom while they were on vacation. My older brother and I went to Hawaii after it happened to help my dad. My Dad's brother Earl and Leigh were already there while his brother Walter stayed behind to look into hospital care and therapy. We didn't understand why it happened, but we knew my dad was very sick and needed us. My brother and I, along with my uncle Earl, stayed in Hawaii for a month with Dad until other arrangements for his care were made. I was only sixteen at the time. My oldest sister was twenty-three and my younger brother was only eight. The world as we knew it had just abruptly came to a halt. Each of us has our own memories of this difficult time in our lives. My brother Wally remembers waking up the morning after mom's death in a cold sweat and seeing her in the corner of the room. He knew right away that she was dead and he also knew how she died. He didn't know what to think or how to handle his experience. All he knew for sure was the vision left him feeling frantic and out of control while at the same time compelled with an urgent need to keep us all together. He knew we needed to stick together because he knew something terrible had happened. A day a half later we found out about mom.

My oldest sister, Jo-Anne was the first of us kids to talk to Dad. She started working with dad when she was twelve and she had an especially close bond with him. Work was my dad's main focus and Joanne worked side by side with him doing the accounting and bookwork for his business. She became a trusted confidant to my dad. Dad needed to talk to us to make sure we were still alive and he knew Jo-Anne would be there for him. He has told us all the only thing that kept him going in the weeks and months to follow was by repeating our names over and over again - Jo-Anne, Wally, Sharon, David, Paul. Dad was found not guilty by reason of insanity and within a year he was back at home. He would never be himself again, but with medication and psychiatric care he was able to function. The next few years were the toughest my family has ever had to face. Trying to move on with our lives, helping dad and trying to heal. But how do you heal something like that?

Ten years later, we heard about an English medium named David Young and how he made contact with people on the other side. The possibility of contact from mom had us all nervous and excited. So the five of us, my two brothers, my two sisters and myself went for readings with David. Our first visit with David was full of emotion. We were in a state of disbelief and awe as the things that David said and knew were only things mom knew. After our visit we all sat in the park crying and sharing the things we had heard from mom. The validations we each received were so powerful we left knowing mom was with us all. As the years went on, we found ourselves visiting with mom (through David) about once a year.

A few weeks before one of David's next visits to Vancouver Island, I had a dream that my mom was telling me that she wanted dad to see David Young. In the dream, we were at my brother-in-laws mom's house and she was hosting David Young for a few days while he did readings. At the time of my dream the two had never met. However, a few days later she met and was quite impressed by him. She invited David to stay at her house and do readings for people. He agreed and was scheduled to come two weeks later.

Now I never in a million years thought that my dad would actually go, but I phoned him and told him about David Young anyway and much to my surprise, he went. In retrospect, I realize now that mom was influencing the circumstances to help get dad there. Dad didn't tell us much about the session, but he did say he thought his spirit might see mom again. We all knew he was moved and touched by it. Just before my dad passed away, a friend of the family told us about a dream she had where mom had come to her and said, "Tell Robbie I'll be there for him." We all know she was.

Over the next few years I trained with a psychic healer, Henri McKinnon, and also became a Certified Hypnotherapist. Henri was very well skilled as a family dynamics counselor. It had been about 13 years since mom died and we decided to all get together with him and work through some of our issues surrounding mom's death. It was a big step for my family because no one really wanted to face the pain of this. Henri had us all identify the protective roles we went into after mom's death. He used his psychic ability to help us recognize these roles. I believe these aspects of us were always there, but after mom's death, they became the more predominant aspects of our personalities. For me, I felt I died too, then 'the searcher' took over. Always looking for mom or at least some release from the pain I felt.

When mom died my sister Jo-Anne was three months pregnant. The initial shock brought on the start of a miscarriage and the doctor told Jo-Anne absolute bed rest was necessary for their health. Even though she stayed in bed as told, a month later she lost the baby. The shock and grief compounded with guilt from not feeling like she was doing enough during this incredibly difficult time eventually took its toll. She did, however, get pregnant again six months later and this time had a healthy baby girl.

My sister Sharon, who is a nurturer by nature, ended up taking on the role of mom. For twenty years she looked after my dad—always there when he called. She knows she gained a great deal from this relationship with my dad, but since his death she also recognizes she lost herself in the process. Today she is well on her way to discovering herself again.

My brother Wally took on the role of Father-the provider, and protector. When everything was falling apart with the business Wally was there to take charge. Always ready to stand up and fight for us.

Paul was the youngest and still lived at home. When my dad was well enough to come back home Paul continued to live with him. Paul didn't exactly have what you would call a normal upbringing. My sister Sharon, along with my Dad's Mom (Granny), became the main caregivers for both Paul and my Dad. Those were difficult years for all of us but particularly for Paul and Sharon. Paul didn't feel he could talk about his feelings for fear of upsetting or hurting dad. Instead he internalized his emotions and ended up getting sick with Chrone's Disease. Really, we were all still so young and only in hindsight can I see how far each of us has come.

My dad died in 1999 at his mom's house with all of us with him. Over the last 20 years dad and us kids have gone through so much healing-- so many levels of anger and forgiveness. The courage and strength dad had to carry on living after what happened is amazing. We must never judge a person that goes crazy, believe me, it could happen to anyone given difficult circumstances.

I had a dream just before dad died. In the dream he was saying goodbye to me and he asked me to sing with him at his funeral "yea though I walk through the valley of the shadow of death." I said, "You're trying to trick me". "How can you sing at your own funeral?" Then he waved goodbye with a big smile on his face. At his funeral I recited the 23rd PSALM --it changed me somehow. It's been said that you are not an adult until your parents have died. When dad died we all felt like we were morning mom too. I have since been to a medium and have talked to mom and dad, and I feel I have closure now. It is mom's death that has driven me to understand spirit and to make contact and it is Dad's life and death that has given me the strength to move forward and teach others how to do the same.

Throughout the years most of my family and many of my extended family have been to various mediums. The conversations that take place because of these connections are quite remarkable. You find yourself talking about people that have died as though they hadn't. You start to feel like they're with you. As the natives say, "Our ancestors walk with us."

The very first time I was hypnotized, my instructor guided me through an inner door inside my mind. As I walked in my mind's eye toward the door, I could feel mom's presence. When I opened the door I was overwhelmed with emotion. I couldn't see her but I could feel her. I was surrounded by her warmth and love. The feeling is still with me today. At night I can sometimes feel her presence and her extreme softness as if she was saying goodnight to me. Previous to these experiences, I could not feel my mom. David Young would ask me why I wasn't letting my mom in. I now know that grief and anger blocked my psychic connection to mom. Many people and healers through the years have helped me open up to this and I thank them for that.

David Young was a well-known medium throughout Europe and Canada. David told me of a scientific experiment that he was involved with that was conducted in England with a group of scientists from Russia and the UK to study psychic abilities. While hooked up to biofeedback equipment (brain waves), when David was contacted from spirit a new frequency would appear and then disappear when contact ended. This has also been found to be the case with creativity and musical abilities. Studies are showing that when musicians are composing, different frequencies appear. It seems to show that we are tapping into a different level of reality.

In the next chapter, I talk about the quantum field. This theory sees spirits or souls as sub-atomic in nature. We as humans exist in the physical world and the quantum at the same time, however this aspect of ourselves is very subtle and forgotten. Sensitive people like David Young have developed their ability to communicate in both worlds. We all have these abilities that we can train and develop. Very creative or inventive people tap into this sub-atomic world often. These inner worlds are full of the energy of thought and memories of our collective mind.

The first stage in developing your own abilities is to believe that spirits do exist. That's what I hope the information in this book will do. Next is learning to listen for the very subtle inner whispers from within. On my meditation CD- Track Three, I'll be guiding you on an inner journey to contact spirits. The meditation takes you over a bridge to a heavenly garden. This bridge does not exist in real life but exists in the hologram of your mind. From this receiving station you pick up symbols or messages from spirit. It sounds a little far-fetched I know, but the feelings and messages people get from these meditations speaks for itself. Don't be surprised if you make contact with a spirit guide or even animal spirits. It wasn't that long ago that native and aboriginal people relied on their connection to spirit for their very survival. Dreams and visions were just as real as waking life.

In today's industrialized, large complex cities we find ourselves very disconnected from nature and spirits. Angels, animal spirits and spirit guides are mediums between our creator and our self. Try the meditation on your CD, but also try the meditation outside. Meditate by a tree or a brook, or in your garden. The bridge between us and spirit or our sub-atomic selves, is our minds. So it doesn't matter what belief system or meditation you use to contact spirit because they all work.

The message I want to get across is that there are inner dimensions or heavens full of life. We are connected to these dimensions and unconsciously connect with them all the time. We can also contact and communicate with these levels consciously thereby enriching our lives. The warmth, guidance and love that can come from within are immeasurable. Our ancestors do walk with us and there are angels to guide us as well as animals to protect us. The ancient hermetic law "as above, so below--as below, so above" talks of the interconnectedness of the physical and spiritual worlds.

Native mythology is full of legends of spirits. This culture is seeing a re-emergence of the old ways as we begin to recognize the importance of such beliefs. In the past, scientists have told us there is no definite proof of the existence of such things as guardian angels, spirit guides, etc. But they also tell us we only use 7-10% of our mind's abilities. New discoveries in science are beginning to identify phenomena way beyond the realm of what was once believed possible.

Remember in these inner worlds of mind you are in control. If you ever feel uncomfortable you can stop your meditation or ask for help from spirit. All cultures believe in spirit and reincarnation and that's because it's real. By staying open and connected to the realization that we live on and even come back to earth in future lives, we will instinctively make better choices about our society and planet. The hardest thing to face in live is death, but as the veil between the worlds comes down I think this will get easier. If we ever reach a heaven on earth, it would be when there is no veil between the heavens. Until then a gifted medium can help immensely to relieve some of your grief.

What I've learned in the following years is the more we open up our perception and belief that guidance can come from within the more it does just that. What happens in our busy world is that we are so programmed to look outside of ourselves that we've never taken the time to develop a inner relationship with ourselves. We as humans have senses that are dormant in each of us--the ability to be in a heightened level of connectedness. It's a slow process but everything good is.

It's important to realize that when you work on yourself through meditation you are opening yourself up. As I mentioned I could not feel my mom's presence because I was too shut down. All my trapped emotion was blocking my energy field and closing mom off. As you clear your energy field of old emotions and beliefs, you can open up to insight, love and guidance from spirit. Remember contact from spirit takes many forms and it is our level of awareness that allows us to perceive it or not. My sister Sharon recalls a dream she had in Hawaii that didn't feel like a dream at all. She felt Mom's warm embrace and heard her say the words, "Remember Sharon the healing comes from within." I think mom summed it up pretty good with those wise words.

The Lord is my Shepherd; I shall not want.

He maketh me to lie down in green pastures;

He leadeth me beside the still waters;

He restoreth my soul;

He leadeth me in the paths of righteousness for His

Name's sake.

Yea, though I walk through the valley

Of the shadow of death, I will fear no evil;

For Thou art with me; Thy rod and Thy staff

They comfort me.

Thou preparest a table before me

In the presence of mine enemies;

Thou anointest my head with oil;

My cup runneth over.

Surely goodness and mercy shall follow me

All the days of my life;

And I will dwell in the house of the Lord for ever.

Psalm 23

Chapter 5

Creator Self

*"The universe has
no beginning or end,
it seems to fold in
on it's self"*

Steven Hawkings

Ask, and it shall be given you;

seek, and ye shall find;

knock, and it shall be opened unto you:

For every one that asketh receiveth;

and he that seeketh findeth;

and to him that knocketh

it shall be opened.

Jesus

Matthew 7:7-8

Where do we come from? The words God, Creator, Quantum Field and many others have been used to explain the unexplainable. Every religion and culture has its own beliefs around this. In my studies I try to look at the similarities of these beliefs. The fundamentals are that there is a force or power that created us and our world and that we are connected to this force, or creator, and can unite with it. I was raised Catholic and was exposed to the bible's teachings that God is omnipresent, that God exists everywhere. God has no beginning and no end. The Catholic school I attended as a child had a strong native influence; therefore, I was also exposed to their beliefs. They do not consider their spiritual beliefs to be a 'religion' in the same way that other organized faiths do, nevertheless, they are rich in spirituality with their connectedness to nature, to their ancestors and to their creator. When you look at the two beliefs, although there are many differences their basic truths are the same. One Creator, one God, an omnipotent, omnipresent, omniscient being.

Which brings me now to the quantum field and the new science. The quantum field exists in and through everything (It is the web of life). In the last 60 years, scientists have shown that sub-atomic particles are the building blocks of our physical reality. Everything in the physical world is made of atoms, and when we split the atom in the 1940's we saw first hand the hidden power inside. Inside the quantum field there is a life of unknown complexity and power. In short, the quantum field is the creative force of the physical reality; it has no beginning and no end. Einstein showed that the fastest we can communicate in the physical world is at the speed of light. However, sub-atomic particles communicate much differently than physical particles. In the sub-atomic world, experiments have shown that these particles act like waves and can communicate instantly. Alain Aspect's experiment showed that when two quantum objects are correlated, if we measure one (thus collapsing it's wave function) the other's wave function is instantly collapsed as well. In other words, a quantum atom moves faster than the speed of light. It doesn't exist in time, but lives in the forth dimension.

We have a physical world of flesh and blood and inner worlds of inconceivable complexities that we are connected to through sub-atomic particles. A controversial theory called the string theory talks about sub-sub-atomic particles. These particles act more like strings of a musical instrument and the different tones of these very strings determine their characteristics. They exist in the third dimension and the fourth dimension at the same time.

These string-like particles are not confined to the third dimension. The idea is that these tiny strings compose all matter in the universe including you and me. With this definition science is beginning to see that consciousness creates matter not the other way around.

The theory goes on to propose many dimensions or heavens within. The theory is that these strings form the elements of the physical world. Different strings create different particles (photons, quarks, etc.) they in turn are the building blocks of the physical world. Your brain and nervous system forms neuro-circuits and instinctive behaviors, but we are not our nervous system or brain. We are sub-atomic spirits housed in a physical body. I think our minds and spirits are made of these strings of energy. Hence, we are connected to this quantum field that is also omnipresent. Science that at first separated us from God is now bringing us closer than ever to our creator. Over the last 40 to 50 years there has been a quiet revolution in science with new understanding of the quantum field. A new understanding of how quantum physics links body, mind, and spirit as one. This awareness constitutes a master key that unlocks some of the secrets of how our thoughts, attitudes and beliefs create the conditions of our body and the external world. Through our understanding of the physical world, founded in the principles of Newtonian physics, we see the world as a purely physical mechanism comprised of parts (matter). This concept has been extremely beneficial in helping us to improve our physical lives. Amazing inventions and an understanding of the physical body and medicine illustrate the progress we have made.

Leading edge cell research has transcended conventional Newtonian physics and has found that invisible energy forces, including thought, have regulatory influence on cell physiology. Cellular biologists are seeing that our environment and our thoughts have a direct impact on the activity of our genes. More importantly it's our perception of our environment that influences our genes. Quantum physics teaches that it is our perception that determines whether light takes the form of a wave or a particle.

This is an important realization, because we can control our perception by our attitude. Which is why positive thinking, visualization and meditation can have such a favorable impact on us. Throughout this book we talk about our abilities to interact with ourselves and our creator at a deeper level. The bible says all roads lead to Rome; to me this means all roads lead to a common understanding. Now it gets exciting for me because I don't have to follow any particular religion to interact with my creator. Science is proving we are all connected, that we are all made of the same stuff. Our gods may be different, but we are all similar in the sense that we are all part of something bigger.

The belief that our spirit being is composed of these sub or sub-sub atomic particles starts to give scientific validation to life after death. The body may be separated at the moment of death, but the spirit lives on in the fourth dimension or higher in the space-time continuum. In every religion or culture there seems to be spiritual leaders or unique individuals who have made amazing connections to their creator. Shamans from all cultures connected to their creator or ancestors for insights, guidance and healing. Shamans and native cultures also talk of the creator existing everywhere. The natives teach that health is present when all things are balanced. There are many stories even today of native shamans healing seemingly incurable ailments. They use pray, herbs, sweat lodges and healing chants to create balance. I've been involved in sweat lodge ceremonies and can tell you they are very powerful and healing. Shamans of Tibet talk of the negative emotions we should stay away from pride, hatred, attachment, jealously and ignorance. Our thoughts and feeling are very important to our health. Our inner sub-atomic worlds of thought are the real worlds of cause and effect. For it is our thoughts that we dwell on that go forth and create effects in our lives.

Buddha who lived in sixth century B.C.E achieved enlightenment while meditating under a bodhi tree. He found a state called nirvana a place of bliss. Through his realizations he created a road map to enlightenment. Buddhists believe they should develop the virtues of joy, patience, courage, confidence and a desire to help others. Buddhists place humans at the center of life and believe in self-destiny. A self that is based on being harmless and compassionate, both to ourselves and others.

It is said that when Buddha was first Enlightened he was asked,

> *"Are you a God?"*
>
> *"No," he replied.*
>
> *"Are you a saint?"*
>
> *"No."*
>
> *"Then what are you?"*
>
> *And he answered, "I am awake."*

Jesus also believed in the power to destine one's life by connecting with the father within. Jesus said, "You can do what I can do and more in the days to come." These disciplines all focus on non-attachment to physical greed, and the importance of equality and non-judgment. It is presumed that Jesus spent his lost years from age 15 to 30 in India. The story goes that the three wise men that visited Jesus at his birth came from the east. Along with information from the Dead Sea Scrolls and texts in India, scholars have pieced together that Jesus returned their visit to the east when he was 15 or 16. It is even thought that they may have suggested or given him his name, because it seems to come from Krishna sometimes spelled Christina.

The teachings of Jesus Christ and Buddha refer to our ability to unite with God. Their disciplines were usually based on compassion, meditation, mantras, fasting and non-attachment to physical items. They all talk of having to face inner fears and demons or Satan. A common thread is the importance of seeing God, in everyone and everything. The message is the same - one God or one mind, and the ability to connect with it.

We've all heard the word karma as explained in the east (cause and effect) this may be cause and effect both in this life and past lives. The word karma is from the Sanskrit root word that means doing. For every doing there is an equal reaction. Even as simple as a happy thought creates a happy feeling. The Bible put it simply as one has sown, so shall you reap. The masters knew that every thought had consequences and therefore emphasized the importance of controlling our minds.

The power of our creators seems very real and the Christ challenge seems to be to unite with this power. "He that believeth on me, the works that I do shall he do also; and greater works than these shall he do" All these spiritual leaders teach that one day we will all feel connected to this one creator.

As we have seen from quantum psychics we are all connected through sub-atomic particles. As we evolve we will become more and more in contact with this force. In the mean time these principles and teachings can help us. They give hope that as we open to our Creator, our God, the quantum field, etc. we will feel more whole. The power of forgiveness especially for your own mistakes goes a long way in opening our hearts and spirits more to our creator God. Freewill to choose right from wrong and good from bad, seems to be God's gift. We are all live cells of the body of our creator. Everything is part of this; the stars, moon, galaxies, you and me. We only need to choose our freewill to connect with this and our potential will be as limitless as the universe itself.

Chapter 6

The Bridge Between Worlds

Peace comes from within.
Do not seek it without.

Buddha

If there is anything we wish

to change in a child,

we should first see if it is not something

that could better be changed in ourselves.

Carl Jung

The best way to cheer yourself up

is to cheer someone else up.

Mark Twain

We live in two realities at once, the physical world and the world of energy or spirit. Our minds and bodies are intricate biological and spiritual systems. In this chapter I want to bring our conscious mind together with our quantum or Creator self's. There are holographic energy fields called chakras and meridians that encompass a multifaceted electromagnetic system. This is the same energy system that we objectified as brain waves in chapter one. In this chapter we are looking deeper into what these energies really are. These energy systems bridge the physical world and the quantum world. Most of this we are totally unconscious of, nonetheless, we are always working in both worlds.

To realize this we must first comprehend the dynamics of the human energy field. Modern science tells us that the human organism is not just a physical structure made of molecules, but that like everything else we are composed of sub-atomic particles. There are levels or dimensions composed of sub and sub-sub-atomic particles or waves. We exist in these worlds and the physical world at the same time.

The chakras are like black holes of energy that somehow connect us with the physical world and inner sub-atomic dimensions. There are seven main chakras that align with your spinal column. The first is at the base of your spine. The second is at your sexual organs. The third is at your navel. The forth is at your heart. The fifth is your throat. The sixth is your third eye and the seventh is your crown chakra. The energy they produce is called kundalini or chi which are one in the same. The chakras are known as energy systems that regulate the emotional, mental, spiritual and physical functions of our lives. They are like computer databases; each designed to look after different aspects of our lives.

To help us in the process of our enfoldment it is most important to understand that the chakras are doorways for our consciousness. They are doorways through which emotions as well as mental and spiritual forces flow into physical expression. They are openings through which our attitudes and belief systems enter into and create our body/mind structure. Developing more of a conscious interaction with this system is an important key to self-discovery.

Each of the energy centers relates to a particular physical function. They also relate to different mental and emotional states. Each chakra resonates to a particular color and sound. I imagine the body as a musical instrument with seven notes or chakras. In later chapters we work with sound and the chakras. Eastern cultures knew the importance of balancing your energy or chakra systems.

The Chinese have been working with the human energy field since the Yellow Emperor Huang Di 2690-2590 b.c. They discovered a small pox immunization a thousand years before Europeans. The Chinese saw man as a mirror of the universe, infused with vital chi energy. Treatment was based on redirecting the chi in the body.

The more you look at metaphysics and Eastern philosophy the more you see that they new what modern science is just beginning to see; an understanding that we have an energy body or soul that encompasses the body. The chakra energy system is the bridge into the physical world. Meridians are like energy veins that run through our entire bodies. These meridians distribute and collect information and energy that in turn runs our bodies.

Our energy fields are referred to as auras and can be seen by some as luminous bodies of light. Kirlian photographic plates have recorded the auras of plants, animals and humans. Even if a leaf or a limb is not present on the living object it shows up on film. Some people who have lost an arm or leg talk of ghost pain. It is believed that the sensations they feel come from their energy body or spirit. There are seven main chakras, but we actually have hundreds, located all over the body. Each acupressure and acupuncture point is an energy vortex and therefore a chakra.

The basic concept is that these seven main chakras along with thousands of smaller centers regulate all aspects of our lives. They are the brains behind everything. Working with these centers gives us access or control of our bodies, minds, and our lives at a higher level. Meditating on these centers allows us access, much like going on line with your computer.

Following is a description of the seven main chakras and their basic functions as understood in the East.

CHAKRAS

1) *Root or Base Chakra*
   Location: Base of spine
   Color; Red

Function: Gives vitality to the physical body deals with matters of the material world. Matters to do with grounding, stability, security, health and survival. This chakra is very instinctive and is connected to our animal nature.

Negative Qualities: When overworked or shut off negative emotions will manifest: anger, greed, violence, insecurity and tension or pain in the spine.

2) *Navel Chakra*
   Location: Lower abdomen to navel area
   Color: Orange

Function: Procreation, assimilation of food, physical force, vitality and sexuality. Process emotions of desire, sex, passion and love. Creativity and movement like dance are associated with this chakra.

Negative Qualities: Over indulgence in food or sex, sexual difficulties, jealousy, envy, bladder or uterine problems.

3) *Solar Plexus Chakra*
   Location: Above the navel and below the chest
   Color: Yellow

Function: Vitalizes the sympathetic nervous system. Digestive processes, metabolism and emotions. Will power and self-control come from this chakra. Self-assertiveness and a sense of power come from this center. Hunches, gut feelings. It's the mind of your lower chakras.

Negative Qualities: Digestive problems, to much emphasis on power or control.

4) *Heart Chakra*
   Location: Center of the chest
   Color: Green (secondary color is pink)

Function: Acts as a bridge between the lower and higher chakras. Energizes the blood and physical body with the life force. Faith, love, peace, joy and warmth come from this chakra. The heart when in balance produces the most energy of all the chakras and can balance them all.

Negative Qualities: Repression of love, emotional instability, out of balance, heart problems.

5) *Throat Chakra*
   Location: Throat area
   Color: Sky blue

Function: Speech, sound, vibration and communication. The power of the spoken word and creative expression in writing or speech, painting and music. Integration, peace, truth, knowledge, wisdom, loyalty, honesty, reliability, gentleness and kindness.

Negative Qualities: Knowledge used unwisely, ignorance, lake of discernment.

6)   *Third Eye*
      Location: The brow, above the base of the nose
      Color: Indigo, blue

Function: Communication center of the mind, insight, psychic center, creativity and visualization center. Imagination is the vehicle of transformation.

Negative qualities: lack of concentration, headaches, eye problems, disconnected from life

7)   *Crown*
      Location: Top of head
      Color: Violet

Function: Connects us to the divine concepts of life, our purpose. Soul chakra, let go and let God.

Negative qualities: unbalanced spiritual expression, fear and paranoia.

If our chakras are not functioning properly it usually results in physical or mental fatigue. The interplay of our chakras, meridians and physical body is just starting to be understood by western medicine. Eastern cultures have long known the importance of these systems. Meditation is a link to consciousness; it stimulates chakras, which measurably increases energy coming from them. The heart produces the most energy of all the chakras and when in balance can send that energy to all parts of your being.

If one of your body's chakras or meridians isn't working right in you, it can produce body tension and illness. Each chakra has specific functions on the physical, mental, emotional and spiritual level. Ancient systems of healing understood the importance of balancing these systems. For example the use of yoga and tai chi are designed to work with these energy systems. If you are experiencing physical or emotional discomfort; it is possible through intention, breath and visualization to clear these energies. If you experience a lot of discomfort, naturally you should see a physician, but for daily tension or emotional issues meditation works wonders.

It's been shown that meditation changes our brain waves. As our brain waves slow down we are synchronizing our frequencies to light and sound waves. When we sleep this happens automatically, but we need time throughout the day when we can recharge our batteries. On track four of your CD I've designed a healing meditation using color and breath. Breath is the energizer of the body and with color and intention makes a powerful tool for healing.

In the meditation I'll have you breathing energy and color to different parts of the body. The breath and energy of color will balance your body's electromagnetic system, as it does it may stir up negative energy or emotions that have been trapped in your field. By releasing, I mean if there are incomplete emotional issues involving grief or anger, these emotions will start to surface. Just allow yourself to feel your emotions in a safe environment. Like crying in the bath and breathing deeply as you imagine yourself cleansing the emotions through your body. If you feel a lot of anger running or walking are excellent releases.

Releasing emotion is a natural part of the healing process and shouldn't be repressed. However if it seems to be overwhelming, you can stop the process at any time. There are many well-trained professionals that can help you in this field.

This meditation is focused on balancing your chakras and energy fields. I use the metaphor of a flower opening up to illustrate the simplicity of a natural process unfolding. Experiencing the simple needs of the plant, as it's processes water and light into energy to grow.

We are not all that much different. This meditation shows you how you can increase energy flow through relaxed imagery and breath. We also pull energy in from our sun. We too need light to be healthy. Unknowing we can suffer from light starvation. You've probably heard of people developing Sad. Sad is a result of not enough sunlight. A little sunlight every day does wonders for our health. In Sweden a light dome has been created that projects a very powerful light externally through isolated rays of the visible spectrum with high resolution. You can only go in the dome for fifteen minutes a month because of its strength, but it's shown that the light regenerates nerve tissue and inter-neural connections. Natural light contains what is called the full spectrum of light. In other words, natural light has all seven colors of the rainbow. Indoor light doesn't, and therefore doesn't provide the necessary energy we need. It's very important to be outside for 45 minutes to an hour everyday.

In this chapter, I've also included a list of colors and their qualities. You can make your own meditation using different colors. Using color in your quick fix meditation throughout the day is a great tool. The psychology of color has been around for a long time. McDonalds Restaurants used bright colors like red because they wanted you to buy your food and then leave the restaurant. Today they have a lot more competition and have softened their colors to blues and greens to encourage you to stay longer. Experiment with color in your clothing and environment. A can of paint can change the whole feel of a room.

Colour:

Red: *strength, energy, vitality,*

Orange: *uplifting to the nervous system, energy*

Yellow: *nerve builder, courage, peace*

Green: *increases vitality, restores balance*

Blue: *calming, reduces fevers, invites relaxation*

Violet: *soothes, relieves tension and induces sleep*

Indigo: *purifies, releases eye and ear tension*

Purple: *stimulates digestion, comforting*

Rose or Pink: *relief of stress and grief, loving, soft*

White: *truth, purity*

Chapter 7

Fiery Awakening

Faith is taking the first step

even when you don't see the whole staircase.

Dr. Martin Luther King Jr.

Darkness cannot drive our darkness;

only light can do that.

Hate cannot drive our hate;

only love can do that.

Dr. Martin Luther King Jr.

To love oneself is the beginning

of a life long romance.

Oscar Wild

In the spring of 1993 I had another life changing experience. By this time in my life I had established a firm belief in life after death. My many visits to see the medium David Young had made me realize mom still existed in some reality. Although this helped me immensely with my grieving process, I still had a long way to go. I started getting involved in seminars that focused on emotional healing and intuitive development. Much of the work that took place at these seminars was to help people move through emotional blocks. These seminars were unique environments for people to explore themselves at deep levels. During this process people would find themselves releasing deep emotion, pain, grief and anger. I witnessed amazing transformations in people in the course of my time involved with these groups.

I learned that trapped emotion in our body and minds blocks our natural energy and stops our creativity. Emotional releases such as crying and screaming were not unusual at these seminars and I found myself experiencing just such a release one remarkable afternoon. It began like this. The format was familiar, first meet and introduce ourselves. Then our instructor picked a buddy for everyone. These two people then become buddies for the duration of the workshop. A buddy is someone who you will get support from, share your feelings with and do specific exercises with over the course of the week.

The anticipation in the group was already beginning to build. As the instructor drew the names it was becoming clear that the buddies picked were already all seated next to each other. During his many years of facilitating workshops, he had never had this happen. Things were definitely getting off to an interesting start. The possibilities of what could happen always intrigued me and this was no exception. The morning was familiar, getting to know each other, a guided meditation that sort of thing. However, at about three in the afternoon I started to feel intense energy in my chest. There is no way to explain it other than my chest felt like it was going to explode. I found myself thinking of an initiation ceremony a local native carver had told me of. During this ceremony one enters into the center of the room known as a lodge. There they would scream and yell until all emotion was drained from them. By doing this they would then be able to make a sacred connection with the earth through sound. Consequently, a chant or song would come to them. This would be there own unique song connecting them to mother earth.

Feeling a strong bond with the native mythology, I shared with the group what I was thinking and asked if I could try to release this energy in my chest. I began by kneeling down in the center of the room with my head lodged between my legs. I drew a deep breath and started screaming. I screamed and screamed until I could feel the vibration running through my whole body. Crouching on the floor now, the energy was building so strongly inside of me that I felt as if my skin was crawling.

My arms appeared to be growing three or four times bigger than normal. I stood up and reached my arms into the air sending a spiraling vortex of energy through my entire body. I felt as if I was inside a tornado of energy. At this point I lost awareness of my body. I became a thought traveling through space at incredible speed. I could see deep space, planets and stars as I moved at what I can best describe as – the speed of light. People in the seminar said the energy in the room was so thick you could cut it with a knife. My body was gyrating up and down as sound was coming out. Then I started to feel scared and remember thinking I'd better come back now. And at that very instant I was back. My body collapsed to the floor and simultaneously there was a loud bang in the fireplace as it burst into flames. It was like a gas fire, deep blue large flames that continued to burn for almost fifteen minutes. As I looked around the room, I realized I could see through everyone, they had transformed into luminescent ghost-like images that filled the room.

Next I found myself trying to understand how a fire could start from the expression of my sound. Where did I go when I was a thought traveling through space, was it outerspace or was it innerspace? It was difficult to share my experience with people, although I wanted to, most people just couldn't comprehend such an experience. Over the next few years I found myself overwhelmed with emotion and insights. I seemed to know things that I didn't know before. Mainly about people, I felt like I could look through people. I could see and feel their pain, but didn't know what to do about it.

My research was showing me that all ancient mystery schools from China, India, and Greece as well as aboriginal and native cultures were well trained in the power of sound. Sound is a direct link to our creator self. Sound can produce visions as well as energy. A vision is a strong sensory experience where the unconscious or creator self gives you guidance. Trance dancing is a powerful technique used by most cultures. Long periods of movement together with chanting and drumming allow the body to slip into trance.

The word trance is derived from the Latin word 'transire'- to pass over. Trance experiences are literally an entrance to other worlds or frequencies. Shamans from all cultures throughout time have gone through initiation ceremonies. These initiates would experience painful, fearful, psychologically stressful events to induce chemical changes in the mind and body. For example, Australian aborigines might find themselves being rolled in hot embers or have a tooth knocked out to induce a state of shock. From these states they might have a vision, or a unique insight from the creator. The trance dances of some southern African tribes are designed to produce an altered state of consciousness. In this state they feel num (energy) rising up their spine, as it rises it fills their body. When the num has over taken them, they can literally walk on fire, or handle glowing embers without pain. The belief is as we raise our energy to that of the fire then we are one with its energy. This helped me to explain my out of body, fire experience more. The feeling of energy I was experiencing would be like the num the Africans speak of. This energy is fire so it can create fire. We've talked about kundalini, and chi in past chapters and how it rises up the spine like a serpent, so num, kundalini and chi are in my mind are the same thing just interpreted differently through different belief systems.

One of the many abilities the dancers have is they can see through people (x-ray vision). The shaman can see disease in people, usually in the form of diseased spirits. He then pulls them out usually by sucking them out. There are many passages in the bible of Jesus casting out demons. Luke 9:37--Jesus drives out the unclean spirit from the boy epileptic. Mark1: 32-39 HE cast out devils and cured many. There is something about the word demons or devils that doesn't work for me. I look at them as repressed emotions or negative energy; I think they are the same thing.

Trance states can be achieved in much less extreme forms as I'll teach in the next chapter. However, the hidden power in these extreme methods should be understood. Other extreme methods Shamans use are powerful hallucinogens. There are hundreds of natural forms of hallucinogens from mushrooms to toads. Some species of toads have a hallucinogenic substance on their backs. Licking the toad can give you an LSD type experience. That makes me think of the fairytale princess that kissed the frog and it turned into a handsome prince. Shamans and healers are trained in the use of such things and I do not recommend you go looking for such an experience.

However, many people have had spontaneous visions or spiritual experiences. Many astronauts have had mystical experiences while listening to the cosmic silence of space as they see their planet below. It's been eight years since my experience and this is the first time I've written about it. This was an incredible experience for me and I am happy to share it now. There are many books today written solely about people's spiritual experiences. Since we are becoming a more enlightened society these kinds of experiences become easier to share with others. As I explained in the last chapter our spirits are sub-atomic (faster then light). When I was traveling through space, I now believe I was taking a ride on my spirit and when the journey was over the energy or the chi released started the gas-like fire.

At this time in my life I feel compelled to explore sound and trance at a deeper level. Many people I've talked to have had some sort of spiritual experience and as we move into the new millennium I think this will be happening more and more. My advice to you if you have had such an experience is to find someone you can share it with. Someone who believes in the changes we are all going through. We all need to feel connected and also to learn from one another's experiences.

Chapter 8

Sound Advice

Kind words can be short and easy to speak,

but their echoes are truly endless.

Mother Theresa

Music is a moral law.

It gives soul to the universe,

wings to the mind,

flight to the imagination,

and charm and gaiety to life

and to everything.

Plato

Edgar Cayce a famous psychic in the 60's predicted that sound would be the healer of the future. The use of sound is as ancient as man himself. All cultures and different religions knew the power of sound. The natives of America use drumming and chanting to induce trance. Further in this chapter we will cover numerous types of chants or mantras with a variety of results. The most important thing to remember is the power of your intention.

Essenes are said to be an ancient brotherhood of teachers and healers. Traces of their teachings are found in Egypt, Tibet, China, India and Greece to name but a few. Their origin is not known for sure but it's thought that their teachings came from Moses communions on Mount Sinai. Whether their beliefs originate from Moses teachings or not, we do know that they existed for three or four centuries before Christ.

Among their many healers and teachers was John the Baptist, Elijah and the Master Jesus. The number one teaching of the Essenes is 'Know thyself'. They emphasize the importance of meditation, simplicity, prayer, diet and mantras. The ancient seers and saints of India passed down sacred sounds so that humans could obtain spiritual enlightenment. Mantras have been used in yoga as a way of connecting to God, or the Godhead.

In Sanskrit the word mantra is broken down in two parts. Man means mind and tra means to release. So mantra means to release the mind, to free oneself from the illusion of life and the wheel of karma. Chanting mantras creates resonance fields that balance and heal our mind and bodies.

In 1934 Royal Rife believed that every organism had its own resonant frequency and developed a device that could create an electromagnetic field to destroy bacteria and viruses. Rife believed that microorganisms caused cancer. By discovering the resonance frequency of these organisms he was able to destroy cancer 90% of the time in laboratory trials. Rife's research was not accepted by the medical establishment of the time. His laboratory was mysteriously burned to the ground and he was blacklisted.

In this chapter we are going to focus on the power of sound as preventive medicine as well as to connect to different levels of consciousness. The power of sound has been written about for centuries. The Vedic bards knew that certain sounds emitted light. Some of the Native American medicine women initiates were trained to produce light. They were held in darkness and had to produce there own light through sound. I was at Yuwipi ceremony once where sparks of light filled the room. It happened when the medicine man's chanting raised the vibration enough to produce these sparks of light. Researchers are finding amazing evidence in this field; it's becoming understood that the pineal gland has a lot to do with our abilities. The pineal gland is a small gland located in the middle of the forehead. The pineal gland is a light meter and controls puberty and influences sleep patterns. In later life, the gland seems to shrivel up and no longer function, this may be because we don't use it. Sound stimulates the pineal gland, the hypothesis is that the pineal gland can, on a molecular level, produce it's own light and therefore can illuminate our auras. It's like the pilot light on a stove, once stimulated it can ignite your whole energy field.

Remember it wasn't that long ago that we found life at the bottom of the ocean that produces it's own light. Through discipline and practice people have been able to increase their light or aura. When Moses came down from the mountain after his spiritual experience it was said he was "glowing". Christ is always depicted with a halo. The ability to increase our energy field has been well recorded throughout time and now we have scientific evidence to validate it. Ajna in Sanskrit means the sun center and exists between the eyebrows also known as the third eye. Physically it's the frontal lobe of the brain; which is our communication center and pituitary gland. The Om or oumm is the bija mantra and stimulates this chakra as well our entire energy system. This sound and symbol is said to be the root syllable of origination and dissolution.

Everything that exists is said to have started from Om. It is thought to express the one supreme power of the universe. When the Bible was translated from Greek to English the word 'logos' was interpreted to mean 'word' or 'sound'. In the beginning was word, and the word was with God, and the word was God could also read, In the beginning was sound, and the sound was with god, and the sound was god. Science says the universe started with a big bang, a big sound. Sound and the power of music and word have hidden properties or healing abilities. Try the mantra Aum. The a and u blend together to make the sound of o. The mmmm sound is made with the front of the mouth and the lips. It sounds like the word home, but without the h sound. As you make this sound you might feel a vibration moving through your body. As you continue making and exploring this mantra you may have many different experiences. Remember sound creates resonant frequencies and helps your body and mind communicate better. Hindu Ayurvedic medicine has long used the voice to balance and align chakras. This healing is done by the recitation of mantras. There are three ways to repeat mantras. One is verbal where someone else could hear you. The next is very softly spoken and the last is silent. Practice your Om often and in different circumstances. You could start with a breathing exercise from Chapter 3 and then move into Oming, loud at first then softer and eventually in silence. During the day if you're frustrated try Oming a few times, if you can't do it out loud, do it in silence. In time, you will find it's an amazing way to move energy and relieve stress.

Here is a list of different mantras and their application.

There are 7 varied sounds of hum as follows

1. haw followed by hawmmmmm.

2. haw followed by hummmmmm

3. hee followed by hummmmmm

4. high followed by hummmmmm

5. hoe followed by hum

6. hoo followed by hummmmmm

7. hum followed by hummmmmm.

The droning and humming of the mmmmmm will follow easily with practice. It is said that this mantra produces a beautiful voice in time. The next exercises on sound are quite different. These exercises are based on listening. Have you ever heard a high-pitched sound in your head. This is the sound of your nervous system and when you are under stress it gets louder. Find a quite spot, use the meditative techniques you've learned and guide yourself into a relaxed state. There should be no background music and as little outside distractions as possible. Focus your attention on the sounds inside your head, you will be amazed to hear not one sound, but two. You can actually hear the pitches from the left and right hemispheres of your brain. Breathe into these sounds and explore how you can direct or change them with your intention.

As you listen to these sounds you can start humming. This creates a sonic anchor that helps to balance your hemispheres.

With practice people are able to become sonically aware, rather than dominantly visual. We actually have a chakra in the back of our heads connected to the reptile brain. This chakra was used more in primitive survival, but can be activated with attentive listening and meditation. The more we develop our other senses the more these chakras open up. Experiment with sound on your own. Try chanting, singing, toning, drumming even screaming out at the top of your lungs. Sound is a direct link to our creator. From the study of quantum physics as I explained in Chapter 3, re the string theory, sub-atomic and sub-sub-atomic particles act as waves. These waves respond to sound; as we chant or invoke mantras we are calling these energies to and through us. I believe that quantum physics is now validating what ancient cultures have called chi, num, or kundalini energy.

It is time to explore these cultural beliefs and tools. The next exercise is designed to align your chakra system. Read the exercise over and practice the mantra for each chakra several times. Then bring it all together starting with the base chakra and moving slowly up to the crown chakra. The sound for the Root chakra is UH. Repeat the sound until you feel the vibration in your buttocks.

Next is the sound OOO felt in the sexual chakra.

OH is felt in your solar plexus.

AHH is your heart

Eye is for your throat

AYE or OM for your third eye and

EEE is for your crown chakra.

OHM or AUM for all or as a completion.

Here is an exercise for release from pain. Pain can quite often be released through sound. My first experience with this was during a seminar a doctor acquaintance of mine was putting on. During the seminar I developed a headache. I was told to make the sound I thought my headache represented. The moment that I hit a particular sound my headache disappeared. The following is an exercise you can try. Standing or sitting make the ah or ou sound. As you make the sound focus on your pain. Breathe and continue to make these sounds, using your intuition allow the sound to change as it will. If the pain is acute try ay or ee sounds. It takes a few minutes of toning for the pain to change or go away. The pain my not go away totally but it will always change or decrease. This method is extremely effective to release stress and tension. Pain or chronic pain may need more of a therapeutic approach.

As I've mentioned in previous chapters quantum physics teaches us that the fundamental elements of nature are sub-atomic particals. These particles are vibrating strings of energy with different frequencies or tones. The Greek philosopher Plato said, a stone is frozen music, frozen sound. Sound is a bridge between our spirit and matter. The sound ahhhh is strongly associated with the heart chakra. As you make the sound you can feel the vibration in the middle of your chest.

The Christians tone Amen, chanted as ahhhhh-mennn. As you can see ancient worlds and religions had some knowledge about the healing and mystical powers of sound and music. The Greek god Apollo is the god of music and medicine. Apollo is often depicted playing the lyre to cure the sick. We've seen that modern science is discovering this same power of sound and music. Specially designed sounds have been used to induce plants to ingest nutrients at many times faster then normal rates. The results have shown huge increases in the plants growth.

The Guinness book of world records states Dan Carlson used special sound devices to grow a house plant 1300 feet high. We know that sound can break glass. There is an interesting story in the bible about the walls of Jericho coming tumbling down. The theory is that with the use of chanting the invading army created a resonance field that imploded the stone walls. With all these things being possible, it should also be possible to use toning and sound to release stress and to help us feel more whole.

Practice making sound in your car, in the shower, when you are tense or if you have a headache. You can create a formal time for chanting as well. My intention in this chapter is to get you excited about the power and possibilities of sound. I was working as a hypnotherapist when I started introducing the use of sound (toning) with my clients. I've also done some seminars that involved experiments with sound. One in particular is most memorable to me. On the last day of a five day seminar I did, a group of us went to the top of Mt.Zouhaliem in Duncan B.C. It's considered to be a sacred mountain by the local natives and has many myths and stories surrounding it. I was standing on one of the mountains cliffs admiring the beautiful valley below me. The power of the moment inspired me to start chanting. The words 'I'm free, I'm free soon replaced my chants. I found myself yelling 'I'm free', 'I'm free' over and over again. Eventually I could feel energy building up around my hands in much the same way as the day of my fire experience. Trusting my intuition, I asked one of the participants who was experiencing back and shoulder pain if I could use this energy to work with her. I put my hands on her shoulders and closed my eyes continuing to make sound whenever it felt right. I yelled, "I call upon the power of the eagle". At that same moment I felt a rush of energy come down my arms, into my hands, out of my body and into her shoulders. She responded by saying that she felt the energy come in, go through her body and release all down her back. We both had our eyes closed but the others watching said that when I called upon the power of the eagle, two eagles appeared and circled low, over and around the group. They circled over us in a counter clockwise direction for a few minutes. The native's say if the eagles are circling counter clockwise it symbolizes healing medicine. Then as if knowing their presence was no longer necessary, they soared off into the distance. I wish I would have seen them but knowing they were there helped confirm my belief in the power of sound and energy healing. Once again, the experience left me excited and intrigued. There is an infinite potential in all of us yet to be discovered and universal energy at our finger-tips waiting to be engaged.

Chapter 9

Back to Basics

While we are postponing,

life speeds by.

Seneca (3BC - 65AD)

Always bear in mind

that your own resolution to succeed

is more important than any other.

Abraham Lincoln

Now lets get back to basics. A lot of what I've taught about doesn't mean anything if our bodies don't feel right. In this chapter, I want to cover some basic exercises that we can do most anywhere. They involve basic stretching and massage, but with great benefits. As I've mentioned in past chapters, there are energy veins in the body called meridians. Along the meridians are acupressure points that act like valves. By applying light pressure to these points we can relieve blockages.

Acupressure and acupuncture have been in use in China for centuries. Their healing system, although complex, comes down to balancing the energy in the body. Preventive medicine at it's best. The exercises I've included in this book are all focused on preventive medicine. They are not hard exercises to do and can be quite enjoyable. The key is to sell ourself on the importance of doing them.

We live in a different world today than our ancestors did, no better or worse, but definitely different. Our stress doesn't come from the threat of a wild animal or fear of lack of food or shelter. We are wired into a global world where we worry about nuclear war and terrorism. Stress comes from a bad day at work or a fight with a friend or relative. The Dali Lama says that in the east disease comes from bad water or viruses like aids. While in the west we suffer from diseases like cancer and heart attacks, these diseases being more emotionally based.

The cases I've seen working as a hypnotherapist, demonstrate how physiologic events can manifest themselves in the body. One example is what's called organic language. That is when what we say affects us physically. An example of this is--I feel like I'm carrying the weight of the world on my shoulders. An affirmation that in time will manifest itself as shoulder pain. Another common one is--I'm sick and tired of this. Over time such affirmations can manifest literally in our bodies. Different parts of our body represent different aspects of our lives. Discomfort in these areas tells us where we are out of alignment in our lives.

Discomfort in the feet and thighs may mean that you've been trying to run or escape a situation. On an unconscious level messages are sent out of fight or flight. These conflicting messages cause tension and pain. The circumstances of these conflicts are often emotional. Fighting with your spouse or children, conflicts at work or school. These feelings often translate into body pain. Discomfort in your hands and arms may indicate a need to express or reach for something, hanging on or rejecting.

To release stored tension and increase your chi, squeeze between your fingers with your thumbs and index finger of the opposite hand. Also rub the palm of your hand with your thumb from your opposite hand.

The neck, head and throat have to do with indecision causing tension or inability to express or look at problems. Our shoulders hold a lot of tension. Massage is extremely helpful. Using your fingertips in a slow circular motion as you massage your temples, neck and throat while focussing on your breath. With intense pain make sound. Remember sound relieves trapped energy. This exercise is fantastic to relieve tension and open our meridians.

Shoulders and upper back pain indicate too much responsibility or fear of neglecting responsibility. There are many techniques you can use but I find the following exercise very good. Massage your neck muscles with your fingertips. Self-massage is something we do instinctively, it relieves tension and restores normal blood and energy flow.

Disruption in the lower back and stomach usually means frustration, trapped energy.

This is a good stretch for your lower back.

While doing the stretch you will feel tension and pain. Breathe into the pain and even make some sound. Slow and easy as you breathe and stretch.

With all of these exercises use your breathing techniques, visualize colors and make sounds. All of the meditations and breath work along with sound can work together. Trust your intuition and use them all-- breath, meditation, visualization, sound and stretching or massage. These are all the tools you need to de-stress your mind and body.

Diet is another factor that plays an important role in the whole picture of health. Creative meditation helps you stimulate your desire to eat better. Also when the body is less stressed we tend to make better choices. I use meditation for many things, but I always use it to help me monitor my weight. I visualize myself eating more fruit and vegetables. I'll remember when I was young and loved eating apples off the tree. Choose memories that help you get to your goal or create a new visualization to focus on. Remember the flower meditation on Track 4 and how we aren't that different. Our basic health needs are simple. We need lots of water. Remember the importance of down-time. If you remember nothing else from my book remember the importance of downloading. Relaxing every 90 mins or so. When you are not under mental fatigue you make better choices. I think we are all very conscious of our weight, whether we are overweight or not.

What I try to tell myself is how lucky I am to have such an abundance of food around. I don't need to stuff myself and then feel guilty or bad about it. Instead I only need to eat when I'm hungry and enjoy it when I do eat. To lose weight we can't stop eating, we need to start enjoying eating. Taking the time to prepare our food and eating without rushing or the pressure of what's next. One of the reasons religions have you pray at mealtime is that a meditative pose slows your mind down and prepares your body for your food. On a biological level, enzymes and chemicals are being released in order to process your food more effectively.

Water is, after air, the most important fuel for the body. This point can't be stressed enough. Six to eight glasses of water a day is recommended. Try to have two glasses of water right after you wake up. Put a sign on the refrigerator or leave a tall water glass out as a reminder. It takes a few weeks but you will notice the difference. We are 70 to 80 % water and the more we drink the more we cleanse our body's organs.

Fasting is good for the body too as it gives your organ's a rest. I don't recommend long fasts without supervision, but I like short fasts. A 24-hour fast on a weekly or bi-weekly level feels like a mini tune up. During the 24 hours try to do relaxing meditative functions. Allow yourself to feel any repressed feelings as they arise. As we've mentioned throughout, stress, tension and addictions repress our feelings. So when we meditate or fast we're more in contact with our sub-conscious. This is why long fasts have spiritual connotations as in Christ's forty-day fast. Many if not all, spiritual customs use fasting as a cleansing tool to connect you with your greater or authentic self. Once again I only recommend a one-day or even half-day fast without assistance.

The last point is the power of your environment. You may not be able to change your job or move into a splashy house, but you can do as they say in the ancient art of Chinese Feng Shui. Feng Shui is the art of energy and placement. In layman's terms it's redecorating, taking color, sound, water and air into consideration. Changing the color of the room as we mentioned in a previous chapter can totally change your state. A water fountain is good to draw in prosperity and good fortune. Hang a mirror that reflects something pleasant, something that you would like more of in your life. Lastly, keep your environment clean because clutter and mess keeps your energy from flowing properly.

Chapter 10

Future Vision

There are only two ways to live your life.

One is as though nothing is a miracle.

The other is as though everything is a miracle

Albert Einstein

A human being is a part of a whole, called by us "universe", a part limited in time and space. He experiences himself, his thoughts and feelings as something separated from the rest...a kind of optical delusion of his consciousness. This delusion is a kind of prison for us, restricting us to our personal desires and to affection for a few persons nearest to us. Our task must be to free ourselves from this prison by widening our circle of compassion to embrace all living creatures and the whole of nature in its beauty.

Albert Einstein

It's Christmas 2001 and we've made it into the new millennium, however the world is experiencing terrorism and the threat of war. Most of my adult life I've followed the predictions of different prophets, some are amazingly accurate and others are way off. As we've seen throughout this book, things are always changing. God or the quantum field, is working with us organizing events. Spirit is working with us at a whole new level now as we move into the millennium. It's time for us to see our Creator God in everything and everyone. This starts with our self's first.

Of all the prophecies I am aware of, the Mayan calendar is probably the best. It predicts earth on it's way by 2012. The Mayan civilization was very advanced in time-science knowledge. This is how I interpret their basic concept. The Mayan calendar shows that we are completing a 26,000-year cycle. In the closing years of 1992 to 2012 there are big changes taking place. We are in what they call the between worlds (the apocalypse). It's a time of huge change, internally and externally. What once was is know longer. I see huge changes happening in the world as I write this book. We have just had a terrorist attack on New York's Twin Towers (Sept. 11). Large corporations are going broke (i.e. Enron). The earth is experiencing many physical changes i.e. large chunks of the Antarctica are breaking off and melting along with earthquakes, droughts, and floods. I don't know what the end result will be, but I trust the Mayan calendar is right and we will be on our way by 2012 and 1000 years of peace will follow.

The Mayan predicted world terrorism and the collapse of some technology. I believe in the future we will look more towards solar energy and new alternative technology. One of the prophecies says we will rid the world of nuclear weapons by 2012. The second is a balance of power between nations and peoples. Also a slowing down of the economy, which doesn't mean we do without, it simply means we share more and take responsibility for our environment. I believe new energy sources will be discovered that are clean and cheap.

There are technologies today such as hydrogen cars that basically run on water. There are energy systems for your house that also run on hydrogen. There are also extensive solar technologies available. The point is all the answers are out there we just need to make it our priority to find them. As we end this 26,000-year cycle, we are aligning or synchronizing with the galaxy and solar system as a whole. All heavenly bodies have magnetic fields, and we are all affected by solar storms and sunspots. Sunspots are a result of complex cycles and appear every eleven years. This energy bursting from our sun directly affects the earth's magnetic envelope. Sunspots have been associated with fertility and natural plant and animal growth. Scientists have found evidence that the sun is completing a cycle. They belief there are great changes happening on the sun and the earth. The particles from our sun oscillate back and forth from pole to pole, which creates the aurora borealis or northern lights. This is the aura of the earth and you can see how our sun directly affects the energy field of mother earth. Somehow the Mayans understood these cycles.

The earth has a vibration rate 7.5 hertz. That is the same as alpha state. The military has used this frequency to set sensitive equipment for decades. It's a constant, but in the last ten years it seems to be rising. In 2001 it was recorded as high as 12.0 hertz. 12 hertz is the closer to the stages of beta. As the earth raises her vibration, we will no longer have to go into an alpha meditative state to access the earth's magnetic field. As we move into the new frequency we are clearing all our past emotions. It's like time is being condensed, much like condensing a file on your computer. I don't think we will notice the time change exteriorly, a day, a week, a year will still feel the same. However, internally as time condenses all of our past memories will surface. It's self judgment day as we prepare for the new world. I believe as we end this 26,000-year cycle we will be experiencing a lot of past karma.

This may sound like fantasy, but if we look at what science is saying now it supports such a change. Mayans say that the earth and solar system are moving into another time (frequency). If I'm truthful, I believe that. We are not separate self-contained units cut off from the whole, but cells connected to a celestial mechanism. We are on the brink of understanding that the universe is an expanding growing entity that we are all part of and that our earth and world is going through an unstoppable change. Theoretical researchers in Quantum mechanics believe that one day we will be able to manipulate the quantum level. As I finish this chapter a major breakthrough in quantum physics has just been made. Scientists in Australia have successfully teleported a laser of light. It stimulates the imagination with possibilities as we envision a world with such things as food replicaters etc. Metaphysics teaches that we can unite with the Quantum, God or the Creator and manipulate the forces of nature also. As I mentioned in earlier chapters, the quantum field is an unimaginable computer that stores all our experiences and is connected to a collective computer. It is immensely important for us to realize our interconnectedness to all things living and in spirit. As individuals, our thoughts, our actions, and our dreams all have an affect on our consciousness and the collective consciousness. We've all heard the hundredth-monkey story; which explains that when a certain percentage of a species learns a new behavior the rest of that species intuitively responds in the same way. This is our hope for the future; it will give us the ability to make evolutionary leaps. The Quantum or God is going through a change also. I believe that we are to work with our Creator not to try to be the Creator, but to be one with the Creator.

If I compare science to metaphysics, I see that the physical body is made of particles that form a flesh and blood body. This body houses our mind which is made of particles that live at the speed of light and beyond. I think that our minds are made of these light-like particles and act like computers coordinating and operating our bodies and our identity. Our spirit or soul would be made of a fabric of particles that are faster than the speed of light. Most of our lives we are only aware of our mind and body. In this way we feel like physical beings not even sure if we have a spirit. In eastern spiritual training it is understood that we are spirit in a physical body. India has been called the cradle of religion. There have been more spiritual masters from India than anywhere else on earth. Indian people are more open and sensitive than a lot of us in the West. Their minds are less skeptical and more devoted to spiritual pursuits. The masters say the soul is like a bright light and when in the body it feels like it is covered in layers of cloth.

The trick is to get in touch with our spirit. The Canadian Natives used vision quests, meditation, fasting, dancing, drumming and ritual to reach their spirit. In self-mastery the goal is to have your spirit control the mind and body. This is an enormous transformation, as you have to overcome the ego and open to your creator self. This usually means overcoming deep and complex belief systems. For the mind to let go of old habits and overwhelming desires it has to have something it enjoys more. The only thing more enjoyable is our inner cosmic music. It is said that you can pass through the eye of the needle or the inner door by the right meditation. Enlightened Masters tell us that by mediating on the third eye and clearing all thoughts we could spontaneously move into an inner heaven. This state is different than regular relaxation or guided meditation. Most meditations take place in our mind, but messages or experiences on a deeper level of spirit or sub-sub-atomic levels do happen. The more we meditate and open up the truer or higher levels we can experience. To begin though we must use our conscious mind (free will) to connect with our creator. This means letting go of old concepts and releasing trapped emotion. Trapped emotions when held inside become our demons (anger, shame, grief etc.) As we clear, we open up to the energy of God or the Quantum. There are many possibilities for the future as we open up to this new energy.

The bible says all roads lead to Rome. To me this has always meant all paths or beliefs will lead to our creator. Science is now using technology that, when understood fully, will show us we are all the same. We are all wired to this collective force or God. We will see we can all enjoy our own religions and beliefs and have a bridge between them. I see this now in a lot of religions and soon more will understand and respect each other.

The key to our flowering into this new world is through our senses, and opening our hearts. People in the future will be able to achieve what only the masters could centuries before them. We will become shepherds of our planet and peace and love will prevail. I look forward to this future.

All the best and god speed

David Large

Chapter 11

Dream Symbols

Let the beauty of what you love

be what you do.

Rumi

We were taught to believe that the Great Spirit sees

and hears everything, and that he never forgets,

that hereafter he will give every man a spirit home

according to his deserts;

If he has been a good man,

he will have a good home;

if he has been a bad man,

he will have a bad home.

This I believe, and all my people believe the same.

Chief Joseph

The following is a list of some symbols and their possible meanings.

Remember only you know what your symbols mean, but these may help.

Accident:
A warning. Are you out of control in any aspect of your life. Slow down and pay attention to your intuition.

Addiction:
Something is draining your energy. What is draining you? Is it a person, place or a real addiction?

Airplane:
The plane is you. If you're in control of the plane or feel safe in it, it's a good sign. If the plane is out of control or you don't feel safe, then something is out of balance. Look at the rest of the dream for clues.

Ambulance:
Important symbol. Message from higher self. Pay attention to all aspects of this dream.

Animals:
Primitive part of self, each animal has it's own power as explained by our natives. See specific animal. If I haven't listed your animal, look in native books or on the internet.

Apple:
An apple a day keeps the doctor a way. Is the apple in your dream fresh, what color is it? The tree of life, knowledge.

Alcohol:
Depends very much on the content of the dream and your relationship with alcohol. Alcohol used to be called spirits which could symbolize expanding your consciousness. If alcohol is being abused in your dream look at your energy in real life are you abusing your energy in some way?

Baby:
Usually means rebirth renewal, something is changing in you or your life.

Birds:
A message from nature or your creator in native mythology. Need to commune with your higher self, connect with nature. Look at other aspects of your dream, but it is a messenger, pay attention.

Bank:
Universal energy. Look at circumstances in your dream. Do you need money (energy) or does there seem to be enough in your energy bank?

Basement:
As in house the basement is a part of you usually associated with your creativity or your second chakra.

Bath:
Cleansing, relaxation, self-nurturing. Was the bath hot or cold? If the bath was not clean look at your physical and emotional needs, are you looking after yourself?

Bed:
Rest, renewal, healing connection with self.

Beach:
The sands of time, bridge between you and the creator force. Need a vacation, time out.

Bear:
Strong, protector. The bear needs to hibernate. Do you? (look within)

Bee:
The pollinator, one who inspires.

Bell:
The time is now. Balance and harmony, sounds an alarm.

Bicycle:
Represents you, once again, how were you riding the bike were you in control?

Boat:
Your emotional self. Look at the quality of the water. Clean, murky, rough or calm.

Book:
Knowledge, instincts, book of life.

Boy:
Male part of self (inner child)

Brother:
Perspective of your male self

Butterfly:
Rebirth or transformation

Bus:
Quite often bus may be time frames, for instance a school bus relates to issues from that time frame coming up. A tour bus may have to do with the road of life, are you driving the bus, and is the bus new or old. All these aspects are important.

Cake:
Celebration a gift is coming, rebirth.

Cancer:
Negative emotions or repressed feelings.

Castle:
Like a house it represents you. Is it an interlock castle or is it cold and protected (all aspects of your self).

Cave:
Primal part of self you may need to retreat or hibernate for awhile. Also hidden potential.

Christmas:
Celebration, Christ or spirit, family, joy or hope

City:
Shows your whole self, is the city clean and organized or is it congested? Always look at all the aspects of your dream.

Coffin:
Like death usually symbolizes the death of the old. May mean you are feeling closed in or shut off from life.

Compass:
Direction in life. Are you going in the right direction?

Cooking:
How you nurture your self or others.

Credit card:
Can symbolize abundance or debt depending on the dream.

Child:
The dream could be a memory from your past or your inner child, as always it's a part of your self. What does this child want you to know?

Clothes:
Shows the part of our self's that we reflect to the world. What style of clothing were you wearing? Look at the colors etc.

Crossroads:
Usually shows choices.

Crying:
Releasing emotions through our dreams.

Cup:
Is the cup half empty or half full?

Dancing:
Fun, joy, celebration if you can't dance in the dream then the opposite, frustration, etc.

Deer:
Be gentle with your self, graceful, innocence

Desert:
Barren, deserted can also mean the sands of time, mystical, again depends on dream content.

Desk:
How you organize your self, if the desk is a school desk it may be about education or new learning.

Death:
If someone dies in your dream it's about transformation, something is dying and new beginnings. It could be showing an inner fear.

Doctor:
Message from your unconscious or higher self, inner healer, pay attention

Dolphin:
Universal symbol of intuition, psychic abilities and connectedness to the natural world.

Doves:
Peace and love

Drugs:
Look at the aspects of the dream. Can mean you are trying to escape something. Are you abusing your self? Can also mean searching for enlightenment.

Door:
Are passage ways to something, locked doors show obstacles you need to overcome.

Dolls:
Child aspect of ourself.

Eagles:
Strong symbol of your spirit.

Ears:
Are you hearing everything?

Earthquake:
Going through big changes, emotional upsets need for balance.

Falling:
Very common dream usually shows that you are slipping into a deeper state of sleep.

Fat:
In some cultures symbolizes abundance and fertility. Can also show low energy.

Father:
Our father is a large part of our psyche and shows up in our dreams when we are changing our self in some way. Also male part of self. Fatherly advice, take notice.

Fire:
Kundalini, transformation physically, can show that you have a fever.

Fishing:
Spiritual, fishing for answers, relaxing at peace.

Friend:
Important part of self.

Furniture:
The way you present yourself in the world.

Food:
Shows how you nurture yourself and others. Look at what you are eating. Is it fresh, what colour is it?

Forest:
Growth, nature, rejuvenation.

Garden:
Spiritual connection. Is the garden well maintained or does it need work?

Garbage:
As a rule it means you are clearing out old emotions or habits or you need to do so.

Gifts:
Receive something new in your life, maybe physical or emotional or energy.

Girls:
Female, sensitive part of self.

Guitar:
Music, creativity, harmony.

Gun:
Sexual energy, power, hostility.

Helicopter:
Like flying is a positive dream based on circumstances.

House:
Parts of self. Bedroom: Relationship with your self or mate, rest, dreams. Bathroom: Emotional state, cleansing, elimination. Basement: Subconscious mind, fears. Attic: Higher self. Living room: how you interact with others on a daily basis.

Herbs:
Healing, pay attention to your physical body.

Horse:
Power, sexuality.

Hair:
Some myths say that long hair shows increase in spiritual pursuits. I think this is true but short hair can symbolize rebirth also.

Indian:
Spirit guide or your connection to spirit.

Insane:
Overload, are you taking on too much. May show that your mind is expanding.

Island:
The Island is you and the surrounding ocean etc. is your environment.

Ice:
Frozen emotions or fears from the unconscious mind.

Jail:
May be unconscious guilt or feeling of being trapped, if you're the jailer you may have issue of control.

Jesus:
Reflects spiritual aspect of yourself or a message from spirit. Important.

Judge:
Part of yourself, look at your actions.

Laundry:
Washing parts of self.

Light:
Inner light

Lion:
King of the jungle, strong.

Lock:
If door is locked represents blocked energy, if unlocked it is a good sign.

Lost:
Losing energy, unclear, if you lost something, look at the symbol for what was lost.

Kissing:
Connecting with your passion, warmth, love.

Kitchen:
How you nurture yourself and others.

Knife:
Can be used for good or bad. Cutting away at something.

Key:
Doorway or answers to a problem.

Marriage:
Universal symbol, unity of male and female in relationship or with your self.

Magician:
Your hidden potential. Anything is possible.

Man:
Male part of self.

Meat:
Protein, primal

Money:
Depends on how it's being used in the dream, your feelings around it etc. Has to do with energy and power.

Music:
Celebration, harmony

Monster:
Represents fears or hidden potentials, overcoming the monster is the key.

Mom:
Shows relationship with our mothers or our mother's beliefs. Same as father. Mother earth. Nurturing, loving comfort.

Moon:
Fertility, the unconscious, cycles and seconds.

Nudity:
Vulnerabilities and feelings of being exposed, if you are naked in your dream and confident then I think this is a positive sign.

Ocean:
Emotions, great potential, inner feelings, is the ocean calm or rough?

People:
Represent aspects of our self's, re-dreaming is a good way to see what these people mean to us.

Plants:
Depending on the image, but usually means growth.

Road:
The road of life. Is it a clear road or is it blocked?

Run:
How do you feel in the dream? Is it positive or are you trying to run away from a situation or problem in real life. Are there things in your life you are not facing?

Sex:
Very common dream and has many meanings, most common meaning is that you are merging with these aspects of yourself.

Snake:
In most cultures means energy (kundalini or chi) are you afraid of the snakes or not.

Snow:
Pure and clean, rebirth, enlightenment, untouched

Stairs:
Shows movement. Look at the stairs in relation to your dream. In a re-dreaming meditation you should be able to feel if this movement is easy or hard and where it's taking you.

Table:
Means of support. How you nurture yourself.

Travel:
Is it difficult travel or is it easy? Are there changes in your living? Usually a positive dream of new and exciting things.

Telephone:
Message from spirit or your sub-conscious, almost always very important.

Tree:
The tree of life, depends on the context that you see the tree in.

Vehicle:
Always represent you, are you in control in the dream.

Water:
Our moods and emotional states. Are the waters calm or rough?

Whale:
Great power, spiritual strength, opportunity

Wind:
The wind is a force representing change. How is the wind blowing? A strong wind means big changes, a gentle breeze means small changes.

Wizard:
Inner power, magic, your guide or higher self

May the road rise to meet you.

May the wind always be at your back.

May the sun shine warm upon your face,

the rains fall soft upon your fields, and,

until we meet again,

may God hold you in the palm of his hand.

Irish Blessing